CW08925588

Tony Davidson

THE GREEN BADGE OF KNOWLEDGE

AUSTIN MACAULEY PUBLISHERS™

LONDON • CAMBRIDGE • NEW YORK • SHARJAH

A CIP catalogue record for this title is available from the British Library.

ISBN 9781787107748(Paperback)
ISBN 9781787107755(Hardback)
ISBN 9781787107762 (E-Book)
www.austinmacauley.com

First Published (2017)
Austin Macauley Publishers Ltd.
25 Canada Square
Canary Wharf
London
E14 5LQ

Foreword

My name is Tony Davidson and I am a London taxi driver with twenty-seven years' experience.

I've always said if you drive a cab for twenty years you'll have enough stories to write a book. For the past two years I've had to take a break, due to illness, which has given me the time to write this one.

It's not just a book of cabbing stories, because I grew up in Hoxton, a tough area of the East End. When I started the notes, it brought it home how violent my teenage years had been.

Before I did the Knowledge, I did five years in the trenches working for British Gas, with a bunch of characters that provided me with a wealth of material.

I have had many battles in my life, including a fight with the taxman that lasted six years.

My biggest battle, though, has been with alcohol, which I deal with in the final chapter. That was hard to write, as I had to bare my soul. In the end it was cathartic, because the near-death experience changed my life, and I'm still here to tell the tale, which hopefully could be an inspiration to others.

'Oxton

I grew up in Hoxton but in those days the 'H' was silent, like the 'P' in swimming pool. These days it's a fashionable area adjacent to the city, but in the sixties and seventies it was pure Cockney. It has always been a tough area, full of villains and the famous 'Oxton Mob.

My father-in-law said, "Nothing good came out of 'Oxton."

I replied, "Most of my mates were villains or cabbies."

Some people say there's not a lot of difference.

Most Friday nights in my local, the Beehive, there was a cabbies' corner. One night the guvnor said to me, "I got a cab to Barts the other day. You lot should wear a fuckin' mask and three-cornered hat!"

"That's rich coming from you at these prices!"

My earliest memory was when I was about eighteen months old and spent a week in Moorfields for an operation on my right eye. Every afternoon the nurse would draw the blinds and make us lie down. One afternoon I refused and stood up, playing my toy banjo.

"Go to sleep!" I was told.

"No, I don't wanna go to sleep!" I was a bit of a rebel even then.

On the Friday, Mum came to take me home. My cousin Pat, who we called Odd Job, was fifteen at the time, and came with her to save Dad losing an afternoon's work. I always thought a lot of him for that.

'Oxton was a rough area. You had to fight. The weaker kids had a hard time. One day, me and my brother Steve were playing cricket. I had the bat, when a new kid on the block came into the play area with his big sister and her mates. He told Steve to 'fuck off' as he threw our ball over the fence. Big mistake! It was followed up by a big right-hander from Stevie, and those familiar words:

"Quick Tone, run!"

We were seven and nine at the time. It was about a hundred yards to the safety of our block. Steve made it, but I was caught, at the base of our stairs, by the big girls.

As his sister held me, she said, "Go on Brian, fuckin' do him."

Before he could, I struggled free and – wallop! – hit him over the head with the cricket bat. The screams were terrible as I legged it up to our flat where Mum was waiting.

"What have you done, Tone?"

"Come in the kitchen and I'll show you."

From our kitchen you could look down into the Addams' back garden, where the women were holding towels on his head to stop the blood. I thought I'd killed him. Seven years old, the first time I did someone with a cricket bat.

About a week later Brian and his older brother got their revenge when they jumped me in the flats. That night, when Dad came home, Mum said, "Look what they've done to Tony."

There I was: black eye, busted nose and lip. I was in a right state.

"What can I do Lill? I can't go down there after what he did."

He turned to me.

"Well son, you did hit him with a cricket bat and today you've learned something. You took a bloody good hiding. If you dish it out, you gotta be able to take it too. It'll make you 'ard."

"Well… yeah," came the muted reply.

The first day I went cabbing was a Saturday. I've liked working weekends ever since; less traffic and the work's different. It's 'Arrods, Madame Tussauds, the Tower of London and the Zoo. Also the punters – mum and dad out with the kids, having a good time.

I was driving along Theobalds Road a few years ago. This bird was walking along, looking like a mixed-race Amy Winehouse. She had a blonde wig up in a beehive, tits hanging out, little black skirt and boots. I thought, please, it's ten o'clock in the morning, a bit early to be out on the game. Anyway, she saw me looking and showed out. I spun around and, as I pulled up, she asked, "Are you looking for business? You can have me for £40."

When I looked, it was only a transsexual!

"No, you're alright mate. I'm looking for business, but not that kind. I'm looking for someone to give me £40." And I drove off laughing.

That Saturday night, my brother Steve came round and I made the mistake of telling him. Steve is your typical big-mouthed cabbie; more mouth than a cow's got fanny as the saying goes. The following Friday, we were down our local for the end of the month 'do.' I was at the bar when a girl I knew came over.

"Hello, Tone."

"Hello Darlin', I'm just getting a round, you wanna drink?"

"Yeah I'll have a drink with you. How you been? I haven't seen you for ages."

"Yeah, I've been doing well."

"Shagged any transsexuals lately?"

"I know who you've been talking to. I bet he's been down 'ere and told you and your mates to wind me up."

"Yeah, have a look," she said. Across the bar her mates smiled as they raised their glasses to me. Then I saw the funny side. I had to laugh.

Over the years I've watched a lot of football. The greatest player I ever saw was George Best. The best young player I ever saw was Johnnie Harrison. Jon-Jon or 'Arry as he was known, and still is.

At my primary school, Laburnum Street, the last year of seniors provided the school football team. 'Arry had been a regular for a few years, he was that good. The best match came one Thursday afternoon when we took on our local rivals, Whitmore, which had four kids who would later become my mates through teenage years and beyond, and their unfortunate goalkeeper, who became my best mate, Danny Anka.

I remember my first meeting with Woody, Alan Wood. As we stood together on the halfway line, he said, "Like your boots mate. Who's that little kid?"

"That's Johnnie Harrison, remember that name, he'll play for England one day."

I think, at that time, he'd already scored two or three and it just went on. At one point he took the ball off our keeper, ran the length of the pitch, past six or seven tackles, before rounding Danny and rolling the ball into the empty net. Both teams and spectators applauded as he trotted back, with that 'Arry grin across his face. The game ended 10-0, all scored by Jon-Jon.

We had all witnessed something special.

We played together again for Shoreditch. That was some team. Sometimes I played against him, because he was a winger and I was full back. I remember, before one game, saying, "'Arry, I'm gonna be so tight up your arse today – I hope you're feeling fit."

Jon-Jon just laughed.

"Yeah, alright Tone."

As the first ball was played up to him, he dropped his left shoulder. I went left as he spun off to the right. Done me like a kipper! Next time he drops his left shoulder, I go right – this time, he goes left. He had me on toast all afternoon. The only way to stop him was to foul him, but I wouldn't do that to a mate.

By the time he was fourteen 'Arry didn't have to worry about school; we all knew where he was going. He was signed up by Charlton Athletic, a good team in the old second division. He made the first team and scored the only goal in a 1-0 win away at Nottingham Forest, managed at the time by a certain Brian Clough. Johnnie had all the skills in the world, the closest thing I've ever seen to Bestie. But, he was small like George, without being as strong. They tried everything to build him up because the pro game is tough: weights, a diet of steaks and Guinness. But 'Arry couldn't put on any weight. He ended up playing semi-pro before doing the Knowledge and joining my growing list of mates as a cabbie.

When we were kids, me and Steve spent a lot of time with Mum's parents, Nan and Farve. They both had some great stories to tell. Farve loved the army and had seen active service in India and Ireland during the troubles of the twenties. Nan said when times were hard they'd run up the rent, then do a moonlight flit to another gaff.

At one place they were skint when the landlord came round. She said, "I can't pay this, the old man's died, come in and have a look."

14

She got Farve to lay on a table in the front room and covered him with a sheet. The landlord poked his head round the door.

"Oh, you poor woman! Don't worry about the rent. I'll see you in a couple of weeks."

By the time he came back, they'd moved on again. At another place, the fella next door kept chickens. When he was at work, Nan would tempt them over with scraps of bread then – whoosh! She'd have one over the fence, wring its neck, have it plucked, cleaned and in the oven before you could say Jack Robinson!

One night the fella said, "I don't know what's happening to my chickens, another one has gone missing today."

And the smell of chicken stew was wafting from Nan's kitchen.

When Farve left the army, he came home to the Depression. He had to line up early every morning down the docks, hoping for a day's work, as by now he had young mouths to feed. He had to flog his balls off to ensure he'd get picked the next day. Come Friday night, Farve and his mates had to take the gangerman down the pub and buy his beer all night to make sure he'd pick them again on Monday morning. Eventually, Farve got a job with the local gas company. During the Blitz, there he was fixing broken mains, some on fire, as bombs fell all around. Can you imagine it?

One night, as they worked, Farve looked up. In the searchlight he saw a parachute coming down near Moorfields in the City Road. He grabbed a pitchfork and ran over to catch the German bastard. As he got closer he looked up again. To his horror, he saw it wasn't a pilot, it was a fuckin' landmine! Farve legged it, just in time, before it took out two blocks of houses.

Early next morning, my Dad and one of his mates went round to have a look. He said there were still dead bodies of women and children lying in the road, a sight he never forgot.

I'll never forget 1970. In May that year I saw Chelsea win the cup for the first time, but the year ended sadly. On December 12th, Farve collapsed and died of a heart attack. I was twelve at the time. For the first eight years or so, I'd known him as the kindest man I'd met. He was a hard man in his younger days, but he'd mellowed and was loved by everyone. It's always tough to lose someone, but worse at that time of year. Farve was laid to rest a week before Christmas. It was the first really bad thing to happen in my life. Nan and Farve had always come to us for Christmas and Mum laid out a lovely dinner, as usual, but as she sat down we all looked at each other and burst into tears.

I met my second wife, Sharon, down the Mayfair, the old Tottenham Royal, and I'd been seeing her for about a month. One Friday night, I was working and she had gone down there with her mates. That night Woody's youngest brother Deano was in the pub. He reminded me of Micky Pearce out of Only Fools and Horses; he had more front than Selfridges. That night he tried his luck with Sharon.

"Cos where I'm from they're all right 'ard nuts. You heard of the 'Oxton boys?

"Yeah, my fella comes from 'Oxton."

"Wos his name? I might know him?"

"Tony Davidson."

She told me later that she thought he was going to shit himself.

"Forget everything I said. My name's not really Dean Wood and I don't come from 'Oxton."

"Who are you? The local villain?"

"No, he might've heard some stories about me, that's all."

I told the boys about it and we had a good laugh. The following Friday we were down at the Horns, in Shoreditch.

I asked Woody, "Is Deano coming down tonight?"

"Yeah, I think so Tone."

"Good, I'm gonna wind him right up!"

Later on, Deano turned up with his little mates – I shot straight across the bar.

"Oi, Deano! Come 'ere, I wanna word with you!"

"I'm sorry Tone, I didn't know she was your bird."

"Don't give me that old pony. She told me you were down there giving it the big un. Now look, there's your brother and my mates over there, all laughing. If I don't take you outside and give you a slap, they're gonna think I'm going soft."

"No, please Tone, don't."

I couldn't keep it up any longer and laughed.

"Alright Dean, get me a pint and we'll forget all about it."

"Cheers Tone."

When I started to recall my teenage years, it struck me how violent those times were. Me and Steve were now fourteen and sixteen. One day in school there was a commotion next door and we went outside to have a look. I saw Stevie being led out of class. He was wearing a white shirt and there was blood on his left side. He'd been stabbed. He was fighting with a black kid, Benjy, who lunged at him with a flick knife. Steve was lucky, because as he threw a left hook Benjy missed his chest, but caught him in the armpit. There'll be more about him later.

By this time, me and Steve had been in a few scrapes and it was like the old Beach Boys' song; the bad guys knew us, and they left us alone.

But there was always the 'Oxton mob, who had some good nicknames: Pudsey Johnson, and his older brother Prima who was mixed race, lean and mean as a scrapyard dog, Jesse James, Twiggy Lewelyn, Binsey Chark and, my favourite, Buster Willy.

Buster was six foot tall, shaved head, white sheep-skin, Levis ending just below the knee, where his high leg Doc Martins began; the original skinhead!

About this time our ol' fella said, "Right, you like a fight? Go join the boxing club."

He's always been a wise ol' dog, and knew the training and discipline would do us good, keep us out of trouble and show the crowd our particular talents, which would earn us more respect.

Together with two brothers, David and Billy Cove who lived upstairs in our flats, we formed the backbone of a good team. Steve was the captain. David Cove was a lovely young fella, but Billy his older brother was one vicious bastard! He liked hurting people, but was good to have as a mate.

The club, St Monica's in Hoxton Square, was like something out of a Jimmy Cagney movie. Adjacent to the Catholic Church, it was organised by the priest, Father Murphy. The team was run by a local Irish businessman, a rogue called Tom O'Conner, and two trainers, Bill Downey and Danny Fabioni. In my class at school there was a gang of six real nasties. The ringleader was John Dunlop, whose old man was a villain down Hackney Road. Dunlop was a flash bastard with a big mouth, but he couldn't back it up. I'd seen a few of the real hard nuts sort him out, with fights always ending the same way, him getting a good hiding before shouting,

"Okay, let's shake."

At the end of each term, kids would get 'egged', but no one had ever egged me.

One day they asked, "What would you do, Tone, if you got egged?"

"Try it and see."

"What's wrong with you? Can't you take a yolk?"

They were having a dig at me, but I wouldn't give in to that little mob. Once outside, they were waiting.

"Come on then," I told them. "I'm on my own and there's six of you. Sort of odds you like, but if you give me a kickin', when I come back I'll put each one of you in hospital, and you know I'll do it."

They started passing the egg to each other.

"You do it."

"No, you do it."

In the end someone said, "Alright Tone, we'll let you off."

I laughed, "Let me off? I don't think so, you're just a bunch of c**ts!"

As I walked off, I thought I'd have to show them that they just don't fuck with me. I knew I could do Dunlop in or out of the ring. Him and two of his crew had started training at the club, but had never actually fought a proper match. One night we were sparring when I saw that some of the 'Oxton boys who knew him had crept upstairs to the gym to watch. I could hear them, "Go on John! Go on my son!"

I thought it was time to put on a show. I'd been training a few months and was getting in shape. I opened up on Dunlop and gave him a bit of a pasting. They went suddenly quiet, and slipped back downstairs.

The night after the egg incident was training night. As they left, I followed them out with Steve and Billy Cove. They turned left.

"We're coming your way tonight," I warned them. "We're going round my cousins."

Halfway across the square, I dropped my kitbag and hit Dunlop with a strong right-hander, knocking him up against the fence. His mate, Docherty, jumped on my back but Billy pulled him off and gave him a slap.

"You're next," I said, before piling into Dunlop.

Soon came the usual shout, "All right, let's shake! Let's talk about it."

"Talk about it? You took the piss out of me."

I turned around, "Right come on, Doc."

He looked at Billy. "Nah, not with him 'ere."

"He ain't gonna do anything. I'm gonna do the fuckin' three of you, one at a time."

The other two didn't wanna know. They were shit-scared of Billy and rightly so. A few years later he was put away for attempted murder.

That night I didn't get much sleep. I'd have to face them tomorrow – or the next day. In the morning, Mum brought me my usual cup of tea and bacon sandwich, but I couldn't face it.

"What's the matter, Tone, don't you feel well?"

"No Mum, my stomach's a bit dodgy – don't worry, I'll get something later." Probably hospital food, I thought.

The first lesson was art. The front of the art block was glass, with a clear view of the approach. It wasn't long before I saw six of them coming across the square. All I could focus on were those six pairs of Doc Martins. I could hear them talking at the bottom of the stairs. I thought, 'fuckin' hell maybe they've got a knife' and my bum started to twitch.

Give him his due, Dunlop came up alone and as we met, he just said, "Let's fight." For the first two years at Shoreditch I'd been pretty quiet. Now I wanted to show everyone my other side. To be honest, I let the fight go on longer than it should have. I gave him some room before hitting him with a massive right-hander that busted his nose, claret everywhere. As he bounced off the wall, I grabbed his head under my left arm and punched his face with my right.

Again he shouted, "Okay... let's shake."

"What?" Bang!

"Let's shake."

"I can't hear you." Bang!

I was being cruel and made him beg me to stop. Then we shook hands and went to the toilet to clean up.

As I came out, Docherty said, "You done him Tone, you're the leader now."

"No Doc, I don't need a gang – you saw who was backing me last night."

In the weeks that followed, a suspicion of mine was confirmed. The girls liked to see a good fight, and if you were a bit tasty they started to show some interest. To the winner go the spoils.

Back to the noble art, the team was really taking shape. With training and fights under our belts, we were all getting stronger. Bill and Danny worked us hard: once a week we ran from Hoxton Square to the Dalston Odeon and back, with only a few minutes' break at the turnaround to try and catch our breath.

Danny brought up the rear with a flick of his cane. "Come on, come on. Work hard, all time, all time," he insisted, in his Italian accent.

We had to sprint the last hundred yards, then up four flights of stairs to collapse in the gym. But, as the saying goes, no gain without pain!

We were registered with the ABA, but Tom would take us anywhere there was a show on. On more than one occasion he gave us false names if the home club weren't ABA. He didn't worry about things like that, he just wanted us to have as many bouts as possible; but I'm sure he made a nice few bob on the side.

One time, we took on the ATC – Air Training Corps. As it was only two clubs, Tom hadn't put a charge on the door, but for that night our place was packed out.

"Bet you wished you charged them now, Tom," our ol' fella joked. "Why don't you go round with a hat?"

"Fuckin' right I will."

And off he went with a bucket, like an Irish Del Boy.

Upstairs, I checked the blackboard. Against T. Davidson was M. Benjamin, the – (I'll leave you to fill in the blank), who had stabbed Stevie a year before. What a fight that would have been! But twenty minutes before the fight, it was called off. Benjy didn't fancy it down 'Oxton.

Instead, I fought an exhibition bout with the rising star of our team, Terry Ludlow. Tel was the mutt's nuts. He'd only had three or four fights, but had been stopped or knocked them all out. He was bigger and stronger than me so, before the fight, Tom had a quick word.

"Terry, take it easy, son. If you hurt Tony you're out on your arse!"

We went through the motions, Tel got the decision and we both got another trophy. 'Appy days!

The best fight of the night was saved till last; it was Steve against their captain SGT West. It was a close fight, with Steve just edging the first round, but in the second, West caught him with a peach of a left hook, that put him down. Most guys would have stayed down, but not my bruv; he got back up and made it to the bell, but with the knock-down, West was in front. Steve won on a split decision, but that punch had done some permanent damage.

A week after, Mum and I went with Steve to the London Hospital. After an X-ray, a doctor confirmed he had a dislocated jaw and was advised against boxing again.

One night, a new face came down to the gym. Like most boxers, we favoured crew cuts. This fella was powerful, full of muscle, but had a mop of blonde curly hair – Jeff Jiggins. We always wore headguards in the gym, but as we sparred, I could tell this fella wasn't holding back. In the second round, he steamed in and straight away a whopping right hand knocked me down. As I hit the deck, the back of my head smacked the canvas; it was the only time I was ever knocked out in the ring.

Bill saw I was hurt and jumped in with the smelling salts – man that stuff works!

"Deep breaths son, deep breaths. You'll be alright." After a few minutes Bill helped me out of the ring.

Tom and the lads had seen what happened. He told Jiggins to stay there. "In you go Steve!"

Steve pasted him for two rounds.

"Come out Steve. In you go Billy."

Same again, followed by Terry Ludlow.

After six rounds with those three, he got the message. In case he hadn't, Tom told him straight, "If you ever do that again you can fuck off and not come back. Now get out of the ring and get changed!"

He didn't last long.

A few months later, I had my best night. I was carrying a bit of weight at the time, and usually fought lads bigger than me. As I looked across the ring, the fella opposite was full of muscle and a bit tasty. That time before a fight was always the worst; you just wanted the first bell to go, because then the nerves disappeared straight away, but that night, as we sat there, they put the lights up and in came the MC.

"Ladies and Gentlemen, before the next bout there's a presentation for some of the lads."

They set up a table with trophies and in they came.

"Davie Cove, Kevin Fyfe, the team captain, Steve Davidson!"

Extra cheers.

"Billy Cove, Terry Ludlow and last, in the red corner, Tony Davidson!"

Another extra cheer.

I went back to the corner and handed the cup to one of my mates. "Go on Tone," he said, "you've got a cup already, just steam into him!"

The lights went down, the bell rang and that's exactly what I did. To fight a bigger lad, you had to take a few to get in close. I had him on the ropes and could hear Bill shouting across.

"Upstairs, downstairs!"

That meant two to the body then two over the top."

At the first bell, Bill said, "That's it son, you've upset him, now get him on the ropes and rough him up a bit."

In the second round I got a bit naughty, pulling out all the tricks. I stood on his foot, held the back of his head with my left and hit him with two big rights.

The crowd roared.

"Go on Tone!"

The chant went up, football style.

"Davidson, Davidson!"

At the second bell, Bill said, "Doing good, son, deep breaths. You know you've won the first two, just get in close. Keep your guard up cos the only way he can win now is with a knockout!"

After steaming in for two rounds, I was knackered, but got through the third. The MC announced the result.

"By a unanimous decision, in the red corner, Davidson!"

The place went wild. As I made my way back up through the crowd, I felt ten feet tall! Upstairs I was sat with all my mates, when up came Tom.

"Well done Tony, you were bloody marvellous tonight, son. By the way, you're fighting him at his place next week."

"Fuckin' hell, Tom, do me a favour!"

Nine times out of ten, that fella would have done me, but that night was a one off.

The following week, Bill said, "Just do what you did last week."

But his corner knew exactly what was coming. He held the centre of the ring and jabbed my head off for three rounds. At one point I heard someone shout:

"Stop it, Ref!"

In the third he opened up an old wound over my left eye. As the blood ran down my face, the ref jumped in.

"That's it, son. Let's get that seen to."

What a difference from the previous week. When you lose away, the ring is a very lonely place and I took a beating for everyone to see.

Upstairs in the dressing room, the doctor put four stitches in the cut, which stung a bit, and I sat there battered and bruised with a towel around my head.

A few of the lads consoled me – we won and lost together.

Billy Cove put his arm around my shoulder.

"Don't worry Tone, you done him last week. You win some, you lose some. You'll win the next one."

He wasn't all bad; it was moments like that, which made boxing worthwhile.

'Appy Days

In 1974 me and the lads were sixteen and thought it was time to have a holiday away on our own.

The lads being Danny, Kevin, Woody and Hoppy, the four I'd played against in the game I talked about earlier, the 10-0 result.

So one Saturday we set off from Liverpool Street station, for a week in sunny Walton-on-the-Naze.

There were six of us on that trip, as Kev's younger brother Steve had come too. On the train, one of the lads piped up, "Where we all gonna sleep tonight? We've only got a four-birth caravan."

I said, "Think about it, it's Saturday night, we're down the coast, there's six of us. Surely two of us can pull a couple of birds, cos I don't fancy kippin' with you lot farting all night. Apart from that, you'll be so pissed, you'll sleep anywhere!"

As it happened, when we got there, four of the lads went out for a kick about and me and Woody dived straight in with two birds in the caravan next door.

"Hello girls, we're your neighbours. How's about you make us a coffee and we'll buy you a drink in the club tonight?"

As we got ready to go out, Danny said, "You two didn't waste no time did ya?"

"No mate, hesitation is fatal. Look and learn, my son, look and learn."

That night, me and Woody had a good time with the girls and spent the night with them. Everybody had a bed for the night and the plan was working.

The next night for some reason, Cindy had gone off Woody and turned her attention to Danny. That night, it was those two, me and Paula back at our place.

I put some slow music on the cassette, dimmed the lights, and off we went. As we danced, Cindy reached up and undid the catch on the wall and lowered the double bed. I mouthed to Danny, "Get in there."

I led Paula to the singles at the other end and pulled the curtain across, but left a gap to keep an eye on things.

After a while, Danny emerged in his boxers and headed for the kitchen. I'd supplied the condoms for the week and they were in the biscuit barrel outside.

A few minutes later, the door opened and in came Hoppy. He burst out laughing.

"What you doing? You don't put them on like that, you don't unroll them first!"

At the other end, I was pissing myself with a vision of Danny trying to put it on like a sock.

Paula called out, "What's going on?"

But I couldn't talk for laughing.

Hoppy went out and Danny went back to bed. After a few minutes his head popped up and he looked round at me, I gave him a clenched fist but he shook his head. Next time he came up and gave me a big smile, the nine-thirty from Clacton had arrived at Liverpool Street!

I pulled the curtain across and turned my attention to Paula, but by now she had gone off the boil. The night Danny lost his cherry, I had to make do with a cuddle and kiss goodnight.

The next night things changed again. Paula now fancied Kevin. "Woody," I said, "they've been through four of us. They only need Hoppy and Stevie for the fuckin' set!"

One day we were out on those social cycles, remember a double bike two on pedals with a passenger in the middle. It was me, Danny and Cindy and, as we rode along the seafront, we came to a ramp for the boats to go down.

We looked at each other, smiled, and down we went at full speed. We ended up in three feet of water, with waves breaking over us. Cindy roared with laughter. Me and Danny laughed too: there she was, Miss Wet T-shirt, 1974!

A few years later, me and Danny were having a quiet pint. I reminisced, "Remember that first year we went down to Walton, we went crazy, like dogs let off the leash for the first time."

"Yeah," he muttered. "Looking back, I wish we'd done it a bit more don't you?"

The following year, it was two weeks on the Isle of Wight with Mum and Dad. Steve took his girlfriend Terri, and Woody came with me.

We arrived Saturday afternoon, got changed, and went for a walk.

There were two girls here, two girls there, crumpet everywhere, and with just us two single lads. Steve's face was a picture. We did our usual trick – found two birds sunbathing.

"Hello girls, was that your kettle I just heard? Make us a coffee… etc."

Wallop! We're in.

As we walked back down the hill, I remembered a story. "All this reminds me of the two bulls atop of the hill looking down at the herd of cows in the valley below. The young bull says, 'Let's run down and shag a cow each.' The old bull says, 'No, let's walk down and shag the lot!' If we play this right we can have a field day. You rarely get two girls that you both fancy, but if we take it in turns to choose, we can go through the lot. Let's start with these two, which one do you fancy?"

"I'll have the blonde."

"I'm glad you said that. I like the other one. My turn next."

And that is how we played the first few days. Then a family moved in next door; a woman with her teenage daughter and son. I couldn't help but notice a suspender belt on the washing line, and thought, I bet that's not the mother's.

Next day, down the beach, there she was: the girl next door, lying on a towel reading.

I said, "I'm gonna give her a pull, you alright mate?"

"Yeah, I'll have a walk up the beach. See you later."

Her name was Vanda, a posh sort from Richmond. I used the 'ol Cockney charm and she seemed to fancy a bit of rough.

That afternoon, my eyes rarely wandered far from her big tits. I thought, I wanna get my laughing gear round them tonight. We walked back up the hill and I arranged to take her for a drink that evening.

As we got ready I told Al, "Pull a bird over the club and meet me down the Propeller later." I had no worries about Woody.

When we got to the pub, Vanda looked over the bar and asked, "What's the strongest beer?" She settled for a bottle of Newcastle Brown. By the time Woody arrived she'd downed six of them.

"She can't half drink," I reckoned. "I'm gonna have to slow down if I'm gonna give her one tonight."

As we left the pub, Al was in front with his girl, Sheila. About a quarter mile down the road, there was a break in

30

the hedgerow, with a five bar gate. I pushed Vanda up against it and went to work. Sure enough, she was wearing stockings and suspenders and 'Little Tony' sprang to life.

I asked, "Do you reckon you can climb this gate?"

In her posh voice, Vanda replied, "I'm willing to try."

Over we went. I led her into the field, laid her down in the soft grass and had my wicked way.

The hedge was seven feet tall, and I thought nobody could see us – until a bus went past and a loud cheer went up on the top deck! We both laughed, but I finished the job.

We were a few hundred yards from the camp when we had round two up against a tree. We finally kissed goodnight and I went next door, where Dad and Woody were having a cup of tea. By now, it was about half twelve and Dad asked where I'd been.

"Oh – we went for a walk."

"What happened to your trousers?"

I looked down at my new grey strides, which now had two green patches on the knees.

"Oh, I had too much to drink and fell over."

They both smiled, "Oh yeah."

Vanda spent the next day with us on the beach, but that night, after rumpy-pumpy, she started to cry. Her boyfriend was coming down the next day. When he turned up I couldn't believe it. He was a typical Hooray Henry, a skinny little runt with glasses. I thought he must have plenty of money, or a big dick! Still, she'd had some fun with a bit of rough from the East End.

After that, me and Al went back to the game plan, but Sheila had taken a shine to him. She wanted to see him after the holiday and was talking about getting engaged. I asked him, "What you been telling her mate?"

"You know what it's like, you tell them what they want to hear don't you?"

"Yeah, but be careful, you might get home and find she's up the duff."

Near the end of the holiday we settled for two Yorkshire lasses up the hill, as by now most of the girls had conferred about us. Keep away from those two!

They weren't the best lookers, but had a great sense of humour and the four of us had some good laughs. We were leaving on the Friday, so on Thursday we spent the night with them, talking and laughing. About six a.m. there was a lovely sunrise, and I suggested a walk down the beach.

It was beautiful, the whole of Whitecliff Bay to ourselves.

I'd had a posh girl for the first time and wondered what a northern girl was like. I found out at the far end of the bay, in the long grass, just up from the beach. It was lovely as the waves broke on the beach behind us.

Al, if you ever read this, I'll never forget that fortnight we spent together, cheers mate!

Two years later we were back on the island. Five of us got the ferry then picked up a coach to take us to the camp. With us that year was our mate Mo, Mohamid Ali, to give him his full title. As we made our way down the aisle, there was a bunch of lads on the back seat, a bit pissed and very loud. They tore into Mo.

"Look 'ere he comes, it's Gunga Din! Oi mate, your shop shuts early don't it?"

I was behind Mo, in my shades as usual.

"Hold up, who's this – the Mafia!"

It carried on as we sat down. "I ain't 'avin this," I told Danny, and I walked to the back of the coach.

"Don't sit there taking the piss out of me."

One of them piped up.

"Oi mate, there's eight of us. Who do you think you are? Fuckin' Al Capone?"

"No, but if you want a row let's have it, then we can enjoy the rest of the week."

The loudest one in the middle just smiled. "No mate, we're not looking for trouble, we're just havin' a laugh. Where you lot from anyway?"

"'Oxton."

"Ah, we're from Bethnal Green! Tell you what, see us in the bar tonight and we'll have a drink."

As I sat back down, Danny whispered, "That didn't half look good, Tone."

"I had no worries Dan, I knew you were right behind me!"

As it happened they turned out to be a good bunch of lads and we had a great week.

I went back to work the following Monday but, after that week away, I still had the flavour. I was an office boy then, working for the Department of Employment. I looked around the office and thought, what am I doing here?

The following Saturday, Steve got married and I was his best man. As we sat in the church I asked him, "What 'spare' is coming tonight?"

"There's Ann's cousin Wendy, but you'll have to get in quick, she's a bit tasty."

A few minutes later, there she was coming up the aisle with Steve's mates Vic and Ann.

"See what you mean Bruv, I'll have to dive in before the lads turn up tonight!"

As soon as I'd made my speech and the DJ started up, I moved in.

Wendy was seventeen, just up from the sticks of Bury St Edmunds to the bright lights and catering college, staying with Ann's family.

After the dancing, Vic took the four of us back to Ann's place and, as luck would have it, the family were away. I was on good form and we talked for hours. Eventually, I talked Wendy out of her frilly French knickers! She was the best-looking girl I'd known till then. She was a good time girl and I was up for a good time.

As I said, I was back from holiday and couldn't get back into the routine of an office job. There was a song out at the time called 'Do Anything You Wanna Do' – it captured the way I was feeling.

Tired of doing day jobs
With no thanks for what I do
I'm sure I must be someone
Now I'm gonna find out who

I packed my job in and took three months off. I had a nice few bob in the bank and used that to live on. Some people thought it was foolish, but I thought 'you're only young once', and for three months I had one of the best times of my life – days and nights out with Wendy.

About this time, a new face had started drinking with me and the lads. Little Johnnie had been a corporal in the regular army and was now in the TA with Kevin's older brother 'Arry Boy.

Johnnie was a short, blond-haired fella, as hard as nails. A few years earlier, he'd been stabbed and told me what happened.

It was Christmas Day and the Greek fella upstairs had his music blaring out. Johnnie went up to have a word.

"I know it's Christmas, but can you turn it down a bit mate?"

"Fuck off!"

Johnnie hit him with a right-hander, but he came back at him with a knife and stabbed him in the stomach. Merry

Christmas! I told him I'd seen my brother get stabbed, and we got on well.

A few weeks later, Johnnie was getting married. The night before, all the lads were down the pub for his stag do.

About half an hour in, the door opened and in walked Benjy, with a white girl on his arm.

"Look what's just walked in," I said to Danny. "Please tell me he's not on this do."

"Yeah he is. I forgot –he's in the TA with Johnnie and 'Arry Boy."

Benjy just looked across and smiled.

"Look he's seen me in here with you lot, and he's just standing there asking for it."

"No Tone, not here, there's a pub full of people. There'll be another time, and think about Johnnie. You'll spoil his night."

Johnnie came over and asked, "What's the matter Tone?"

"That's the B – C – that stabbed my brother!"

"I'm sorry Tone, I didn't know."

"John, we're gonna leave, cos if we don't I'll spoil your night and I don't wanna do that. But do me a favour. Tell him I'm leaving for your sake and I'll see him another time."

Johnnie thanked me, saying, "See me outside before you go."

Outside, we shook hands and I wished him all the best for tomorrow. He slipped me a piece of paper and said, "Tone, I know exactly how you feel, 'ere's where he's living now."

All the boys saw what happened and knew I would get him in time.

The following Saturday I took Wendy to a club up West and spent the night at her place. That night Benjy had an accident.

He used to fly around, pissed, in a two-seater Triumph Spitfire. That night, his brakes failed. He crashed into a wall and went head first through the windscreen. Later in hospital the police took a blood sample. That was when he lost his driving licence and his right eye. Shame.

Monday night I walked in the pub, all the boys were sitting at the bar. Micky Burke turned round.

"You bastard!"

"What?"

"You fuckin' done him!"

"No, it was nothing to do with me."

The guvnor, Stan, came over.

"Nice one Tone, I heard what happened. Let me shake your hand."

I repeated, "It was nothing to do with me, but give all the boys a drink and have one yourself."

The lads kept on. "Come on Tone, you can tell us. We're your mates."

"It wasn't me and I tell you how you know it wasn't. If I'd have got him, he wouldn't be in hospital tonight, he'd have been in the morgue!"

It didn't matter how many times I denied it, everyone thought it was me. I must admit it didn't do my reputation any harm, but I started thinking maybe I'd get a pull from Ol' Bill or worse. Benjy hadn't died, he might come back at me; but he never did. I think he got the message.

My next job was for the LEB, London Electric. After a few weeks I was sent on an induction course, where I met my first wife, June. I finished bottom of the class that week because I couldn't concentrate. I spent most of my time gazing at her.

June was a lovely girl with a figure to match. She was as mad as a box of frogs, but I fell for her big time. That summer we'd finished work, then Friday night or Saturday morning we'd drive down to the south coast and find a nice bed and breakfast for the weekend.

One Friday, we didn't go away. Instead, I took her to a restaurant adjacent to the West Stand at Chelsea, on the Fulham Road – Barbarella's. I'd been there once before with a posh sort and didn't get much change out of £150, equivalent to at least double these days, so it was a bit of a treat.

About halfway through our main course, a couple sat down at the table to our left. He was a typical Chelsea type, another Hooray Henry. A bit pissed and very loud. He turned to me.

"Don't you think this is rather a nice tweed jacket I'm wearing?"

"Yeah, it's lovely mate."

"I'm an alcoholic genius you know."

"Yeah mate, so am I."

June told me to just ignore him.

He turned to the young blonde he was with, who couldn't speak much English.

"I'm going to take you home and fuck the arse off you!"

"That's charming," said June.

I intervened, "Oi mate, why don't you just shut up and eat your dinner."

"Cor blimey! I'm sorry *mate*."

The red mist descended.

"Don't you take the piss out of me. Open your mouth one more time and I'll hit you so hard I'll knock you through the fuckin' window!"

June was kicking me under the table, "Stop it, stop it!"

"Are you threatening me?"

"No, it's a fuckin' promise! Now shut up and eat your dinner."

The manager came over.

"What's the problem, sir?"

"He's the problem. You'd better move him, or I will."

They moved the idiot to another table and brought us a drink on the house.

On the way home to June's, I could tell she'd really enjoyed the floorshow. Halfway home I pulled over and she thanked me for a lovely night!

By now, I'd moved on again and was working at the Post Office. Part of the training was learning postcodes. It was quite a lot of work, but I started to think if I could do this, maybe I could have a go at the Knowledge.

Steve was onto it, as was Danny and Hoppy. With shift work at the Post Office, you had the time to learn it; if you had a badge and could get on the early shift it was ideal. You had wages, holidays, sick pay – then take a cab out in the afternoons, lovely!

I wasn't there long because I couldn't get used to the late 10-6 a.m. shift, but I did have a few good times.

My first van collection was a Friday night, and Old Wally, the driver, took us to start the round in Moorgate. I jumped out and began to clear the post-box.

"What you doing? Take a handful and get back in."

We'd gone out at six o'clock and had two hours to do the round. We were back at the depot by twenty past.

Wally said, "You can fuck off now, back on at eight o'clock right."

I didn't need telling twice and went next door to the Penny Black.

My mate Phil was at the bar with an old black fella, who offered me a drink.

"What you want man?"

"Pint of Fosters."

"Pint of Fosters and a large Chivas."

"You've just met me and you buy me a large Scotch?"

"Yeah man, it's me birthday – ya know you can never have too many friends!"

After a few more pints and chasers, I was in no fit state to sort letters, so I had an early night.

That late shift was a killer. One Sunday evening I was playing snooker with June's brother and really didn't fancy going in at ten p.m.

About two a.m. on the Monday morning, one of the guvnors on the floor came over to me and another fella.

"You two, come with me."

He led us to a massive pile of mailbags.

"Right, shift them across to the other side of the floor to the loading bay. When you've done that, you can go home alright?"

"Right Guv."

For the next two hours we flogged our balls off and shifted the lot. He came back over.

"Right, now put 'em all back."

"Are you having a laugh?"

"No, I'm telling you to put them all back!"

"Go fuck yourself! I'm going home, you can send my cards on tomorrow!"

That was the only job the ol' fella encouraged me to leave, and he talked me into joining him and the family at British Gas where he ran the depot at Stoke Newington. My uncle, Billy, ran Stratford, my cousin, Little Johnnie was at Barking Road and I joined my other uncle, Big Johnnie, at Hackney, as a service layer.

The Gas

Before I started on the gas, the ol' fella had a chat with me. He said the job was different from anything I'd done before. Working on the roads was tough, the guys I'd be working with were rough diamonds. In that environment they view you as one of two things: a mug, or a bastard.

I knew a few of the lads at Dad's yard, as they came from 'Oxton. Doris (Derek Day), Gregory (Tony Peck) and my mate Kev, who had started just before me.

Dad had told me stories about one fella who was so obnoxious his men had refused to work with him, and he'd been transferred to Hackney. The clue was in his various nicknames: the Animal, Prehistoric and my favourite – Cyclops!

My first day on the job began with a trip to the café. It was traditional to have a good breakfast before you started work, an unofficial privilege.

There were eight of us around the table as the girl brought up the fare.

"Two bacon rolls; egg, bacon and mushrooms –

One with everything on it!"

She wasn't kidding: egg, bacon, sausage, pork chop, liver, chips, tomatoes and mushrooms, plus a massive pile of bread.

I looked over and thought, I know who *you* are mate!

My ganger that day was Crazy Arfa. As Bert's breakfast arrived, he turned away and groaned, "For fuck's sake."

Arfa never touched breakfast. A cup of tea and a fag was all he could face, because he'd been on the sauce the night before. We did one job that morning, but by lunchtime Arfa and his sidekick, Dublin Bill Ryan needed a 'livener'.

Another tradition was to take a new bloke for a drink as the job could be dangerous and you wanted to know the kind of fella you were working with. We had a couple of hours in one pub, then onto another in Lea Bridge that did 'afters.' By the time we got back to the yard I thought, I think I'm gonna like it here.

My second day is one I'll never forget. I was with another ganger, JJ Murphy, Prehistoric and Robbo. Robbo was an older guy who in earlier years had worked with Dad and my uncles but at fifty-two, Les was still out on the roads.

We did one job in the morning then moved on to another after lunch to re-lay a factory in Homerton, in a small industrial alley, Mackintosh Lane. I was green as grass. I'd been given fireproof overalls but chose not to wear them. It was a warm day and I'd been working shirt off, just Levis and Doc Martins. I was after a tan.

JJ was in the factory while we knocked out the ground outside. It was the first time I'd used a compressor and, in the tight alleyway, the noise was deafening.

After a while Robbo tapped my shoulder. "I'll give you a blow, Tone."

As he restarted the gun, bang! Up it went. He'd hit the electric cable, a jet of flame shot up the wall. I felt the heat on my back and hit the deck. I turned round to see a terrible sight. Robbo was screaming, running, engulfed in flames. I chased down the alley after him as Prehistoric just stood there, mouth open.

By the time I caught up to him, Les had beaten out the flames, but was in a terrible state. He was burnt black from head to toe. All that was left of his clothes were the remnants of his vest and pants.

Two women came out from the factory next door and covered Les with a sheet. Within five minutes an ambulance arrived from the nearby Homerton Hospital. I went with him and he was rushed into A & E while I sat outside in a state of shock.

After a while, our guvnor, Eddie Gatland, turned up.

"Are you alright Tony?"

"Yeah, I think so."

"Well, you better get back on the job then."

I walked out of the hospital but didn't really know where I was. Somehow I found my way back to Mackintosh Lane. Talk about a baptism of fire. I needed a few stiff drinks after that shift, and I thought how lucky I'd been.

At breakfast in the yard, there was a sombre mood amongst the lads. I was working with JJ again and as he set up the gun he said, "Tony, pick it up son. It's like falling off a bike, you'll never forget what you saw yesterday and you'll wear your overalls, right?"

"Right."

We went to visit Robbo on the Saturday; JJ came round for me with his wife and Prehistoric. He'd been transferred to the special burns unit at East Grinstead, set up in World War II by the Canadian Air Force, 'The Guinea Pig Club.'

Les was in a sealed unit to prevent infections and we spoke to him via an intercom. We all had a few words and wished him well. Bert just said, "Alright Les? Getting plenty of grub?"

On the way home, JJ pulled over to a Little Chef for a coffee and burger. As soon as I looked at the menu, I knew what Bert was having. Sure enough, "I'll have the special, Darlin'." And up it came, a massive fry up. JJ must have told his missus the stories about the Animal, but her face was a picture seeing him tear into his lunch.

One of the best times, was when he pulled some old bird and took her to the Pizza Hut at Stamford Hill, where you could pay for one, but eat as much as you liked. He ate so much they barred him! And he never saw the woman again.

What a surprise.

After a few weeks, I was placed in a regular gang of three with Keith McStay and Tony Ivens (Ivano). Mac was the best in the yard. I earnt well with him and if you were willing to learn, Keith would always let you have a go; he taught me a lot.

We were cutting off some old houses due for demolition, when the two of them disappeared leaving me to do the work. What's going on 'ere? I wondered, and followed them inside. I could hear them up top and made my way upstairs. There they were ripping lead off the roof. Mac turned to me.

"Don't worry Tone, you carry on downstairs. Whatever we get goes three ways."

In those days there were a lot of streets due for demolition and we'd go in first to cut off the gas. If we didn't take the 'bluey', the builders would. One fella was the 'king of toot', Harry Cross. One day there were two gangs cutting off a row of old houses. Crossy was going roof-to-roof and started on the last one when one of the boys shouted up, "Not that one 'Arry, they're still living there!"

'Arry Boy always had plenty of dough and liked to play cards on Saturday night, for big money. If he didn't have a good night, he'd make up for it next day.

While most people sat down for Sunday lunch, 'Arry and his mate would take an old van down Kent and nick half a dozen sheep. He'd cut their throats and deliver them to his mate's shop down the meat market.

JJ asked him one day, "Don't that bother you, H?"

"Nah, there's fuckin' money walking about in them fields."

That's what it was like at Hackney Yard; full of characters like a bunch of pirates. We had a good laugh and I earned good money. Whatever the average Joe was earning, we were on double that, with overtime, call duty and more fiddles than the London Philharmonic.

My first six months on the job, though, were rough. After a hard day on the roads, every part of me ached, but in time I got used to the backache, cuts and blisters and the job made you tough.

Sometimes the hours could be brutal. If you wanted to finish at five, you had to tell the Ayatollah (Gatland) by eight in the morning, if not you were obliged to work. Often, you could be finished at four o'clock, then get an escape, a gas leak. If it was a bad one, you could still be on it the following morning, right around the clock, until you were relieved. We worked hard and drank hard too. I ate like a horse, drank like a fish, but never put on any weight, just muscle. It was the fittest I've ever been in my life.

One day I'd been tootin', and went back to the yard filthy dirty. Brian Keeley eyed me, "Look at the state of you. I fuckin' know what you've been up to!"

We called Brian Billy Liar for the stories he told. He'd christened a few of us too: Uncle Mac, Tinker and me, Blue Boy, after the fella on the High Chapparral, because I was the youngest in the yard – being the only Chelsea fan, it stuck.

I was having a drink with Brian, when he told me the story of when he was stabbed with a kitchen knife. He walked (yes, walked!) into A & E at the London Hospital. A nurse called into the waiting room, "We'd better see you now Mr Keeley."

"No," says Brian. "see this fella next – he's worse than me."

I burst out laughing. "Fuck off! What do you take me for?"

"It's true I tell ya! Look." He pulled up his shirt to reveal a scar where he'd had an operation. Priceless!

It was a Monday and there was a new face in the yard, Lenny. You only had to look to see what he was – a big, hard bastard.

He came out with me and Ivano. As usual we wanted to take the new bloke for a drink. He declined.

For the first month or so he kept himself to himself. Later on he started to open up and we got on well. One day, I asked him what was the matter?

"When you started, Len, did you have a problem?"

"Yeah, with you."

"Me, what did I do?"

"It was when you said you was from 'Oxton. The mob there killed one of my mates."

His mate was at a party and had got into a row with some of the 'Oxton boys.

"They threw him over a balcony, six floors up. That's why I was quiet – then I got to know you."

Lenny was one of the hardest men I ever met.

I married June in September 1981. It was a big church wedding with all the works, horse and carriage, large reception, a night at the Savoy and honeymoon in Paris.

We'd been together, on and off, for the past three years. It was funny, I couldn't live with her or without her. When we were apart, I'd go out with other girls, but no one compared to June, she was the only girl I physically ached for.

Sadly though, things didn't work out for us and eighteen months later we were divorced. It broke my heart. The only good thing to come out of it was, now, I had my own flat.

I started drinking too much, to drown my sorrows, but still had a few laughs. I'll always remember the funniest thing I saw on the gas; it was the 'rivers of Babylon'.

It was a dark winter's day in November. One of those days when it never really gets light. It rained on and off most of the day. We were re-laying a service in Ashenden Road, the steepest hill in the district.

Ivano and Kevin, a new lad, were working inside, while I was in the road, drilling a hole in an eight-inch main. It was about four o'clock, dark already. I'd only cut a few threads when it was obvious something was wrong. Whenever you drilled a main, there was always some gas, but this day it was pissing out.

At that moment the heavens opened up again and I was getting soaked. I stripped off the drilling tackle and put in a temporary plug. As I got out of the hole, which was about four foot deep, the hill became a fast-flowing river.

I took shelter in the doorway of the house. The lady came out.

"Oh, you poor sod, you're soaked. Would you like a cup of tea?"

"That'll be lovely darlin'… and there's three of us, thank you."

While we had our tea I said to Ivens that I couldn't make out why I was taking so much gas because I'd made sure I'd used the 8' rubber seal.

As we looked across the front garden, we saw an umbrella suddenly disappear from above the hedge, followed by a scream.

"Fuckin hell. He's fell down the hole!"

Sure enough, this fella had ran across the road in the dark and rain. He must have thought it was a puddle, but – woosh! Down he went. As Ivano helped him out, me and Kev looked at each other, trying not to laugh, when he came out with a classic:

"Look at the state of me, I paid forty pounds for this suit!"

I had to walk away. What made it worse was that I could see Uncle Johnnie sitting in his van opposite, looking on. He had his cap pulled down, and had sunk low in his seat, not wanting to get involved, although he was the duty supervisor.

When the fella finally left, Johnnie came over and we saw we had a major problem. As he fell in, he'd dislodged the plug. We had a hole in the main, in four foot of water which was bubbling away 'woolla bulla'.

Ivens panicked, "Quick Tone, get in and put the plug back in."

"Fuck off!"

Next thing he gets in, takes a breath and dives under. He came up splashing. "Get a plug. Get a plug!"

"What we gonna do John?" I asked him.

"Leave silly bollocks there and come with me."

At the back of the van he said, "Quick, cut the broom handle down to a point and bring a hammer."

Back at the hole, Ivens guided the handle into the main with me above. Wallop! Panic over.

Kev and me bailed it out, then I cut off the handle, flush with the main, and wrapped it up for the night.

As we finished off, Ivens stood there wet and shivering but still said, "Fancy a pint?"

"How the fuck can you walk in a pub like that?"

What a doughnut!

I really appreciated having the ol' fella across the road after that incident. Again, he proved he was the top man. He sussed it straight away. What I had come across was a rarity. There were a few old mains on the district that weren't fully round, more oval. That's why the drilling tackle wasn't sitting right. He told me how to set it up, not by the book, but how it would get us out of trouble.

In the clear light of day, and with a bit of help from Kev, it worked a treat. He was impressed.

"Nice one, my son!"

"It's like anything else mate: easy when you know how!"

A few months later the call gang were a man short; a bloke had gone sick, so I picked it up with Crazy Arfa and Tinker – Vic Gull.

Vicky was a real hard case from Canning Town. Like Lenny you only had to look to see. His face was scarred and he was built like a bull with the biggest pair of shoulders.

As we left the yard, Vic joked, "Look at them fuckin' boots, mind you don't get 'em dirty."

I'd bought a new pair of Doc Martins.

"Yeah, I'm going dancing in them tonight."

After lunch I met them in the pub at the back of the yard – the Florfield.

"Alright Arfa?"

"No, I ain't. I've just had a bowl of that 'Chilli Gon Jarno' and it's burnt my fuckin' mouth!"

"S'pose you want another pint to cool it down?"

He laughed. "Go on then fella. We'll have that, then we better get back."

He'd earnt his nickname a few years earlier. He was working down 'Oxton with his drinking partner, Bill Ryan, when they uncovered an LEB cable.

"Carfull, Arta," says Dublin Bill.

"Don't worry about that, it's dead. Give me the pickaxe."

Bang! Up it went, blew the head off the pick and left Arfa holding the handle with blackened arms and face.

"You was fucking right!"

He had the biggest mouth in the yard, as he demonstrated one day when the guvnors came down for a meeting with us. Arfa was ranting on about something.

"We ain't doing this and we ain't fuckin' doing that…"

John Ord the district engineer picked up. "I see you've got a fine command of the English language Arthur."

"Bollocks!" came the reply. You had to laugh.

That Monday we finished early after a busy weekend (the call gang had to be available from five p.m.), and I had an early night.

At ten thirty Arfa rang. "We got a job fella. I'll pick Vic up and see you in an hour."

The job was in Old Ford Road, Bethnal Green. The air was full of gas, a broken main, probably an all-nighter. As I set up the rock drill, to make bar-holes in the road, I knew what was coming. By then it was midnight and it made one hell of a noise.

A fella shouted down from his window.

"Turn that fuckin' thing off! I've got work in the morning."

"Tell me about it mate. I've been working all day."

"If you don't stop I'll call the Old Bill."

"Yeah, you do that Einstein. They'll tell you we've got a gas leak!"

About one thirty a.m. we found the break. Vic was on the gun and I was down the hole just above the main. Arfa was about ten feet away having a fag – talk about no smoking.

"Hold it, Vic." I could hear the gas hissing. "We're right on it mate."

I carried on digging out the main as Vic restarted the gun.

Bang!

Vic hollered, "The street cable!"

The explosion threw me to the back of the hole. For a few seconds, I was blinded by the flash. Then I was horrified to see the gas had caught light. The hole was full of flames.

We'd piled the earth behind us when we went down, and had been climbing out over the kerbstone above the main. As I scrambled up the loose earth, I was falling back into the flames that were licking my arse! The flameproof boiler suit I was wearing gave me about thirty seconds to get out, but things were warming up.

I'm sure I got out of there on pure adrenaline, like when you're being chased you find a bit extra from somewhere. I sprang up and ran down the road, peeling off the boiler suit. I ended up sitting on a low fence opposite.

"Look at my fuckin' boots!" The soles of my new Doc Martins had melted.

Vicky came over. "Fuckin' hell, Tone. I thought you'd had it!"

Everybody had run when it went up, but Arfa went back with the extinguisher to put out the fire, and got burnt around his stomach. He looked down. "I'd better put my overalls on."

"It's a bit late now fella!"

The call fitter radioed for help and soon Gatland arrived to take over, followed by Terry Kemp's gang from Dad's yard. Arfa went to hospital and Kempy gave me a lift home.

As he dropped me off he said, "Wake the old man up and tell him to break out the brandy. Take it easy, son."

By now it was three a.m. but I took Tel's advice and called in to see the Ol' Fella. Over a large brandy, I told him what happened and I started shaking.

"Fuckin' hell, I nearly got barbequed tonight!"

I had the Tuesday off. Back in the yard, Wednesday morning, the lads gathered round to look at my burnt overalls and boots.

"You alright, Tone?"

Vicky piped up, "He's fuckin' lucky to be here I tell ya!"

I had a quiet word with Lenny. "I know one thing mate, I've been lucky twice. Whatever they're paying me, it's not enough. I think it's time to have a go at the Knowledge."

It's funny, sometimes people in the cab say, "I wouldn't fancy your job mate, you never know who you're picking up. It's dangerous."

"It's not that bad, believe me. I've done a dangerous job!"

In early 1982 I got my own place, just up the road from Mum and Dad. For a while I had the best of both worlds. I'd get home, have a shower, dinner at Mum's then go out. If I got lucky, it was back to my place.

It was a typical Friday in June that year. We'd done a job in the morning, had one in hand for the afternoon and gone for a liquid lunch down the Horns at Shoreditch. It was popular with the younger lads at the yard, because Fridays they laid on a couple of strippers.

51

We came out of there about three thirty, fish 'n chips, then back to the yard for a game of snooker. I got home about six and crashed out.

At nine, I got a call from my mate, Charlie.

"Fancy a pint, Tone?"

"No Chas, to be honest I was asleep. I've been on the piss all afternoon."

"Come on, it's Friday night. You'll feel better after a light ale."

"Go on then, give me half an hour."

After a few liveners back down the Horns we went on to the Mayfair, the old Tottenham Royal. We'd just got a drink when I noticed two girls along the bar. We dived in, bought them a drink and were well away. Little did I know I'd just met my second wife, Sharon. I took her home that night and arranged to take her out on Sunday.

However, after a large lunch at Mum's, I was dozing on the settee.

"Ain't you going out tonight, Tone?"

"I was, but I don't really feel like it now."

"Go on, give the girl a call. You'll enjoy it once you're out."

It's funny how things turn out. I took Sharon for a drink down the River Lea. I remember looking at her big brown eyes and my best emotions were starting to stir again. We finished back in the Alwyne Castle at Highbury. I always liked to go there on a first date, as in the dimly lit alcoves you could have a nice chat with some good background music.

After a few weeks, me and Sharon had become an item. In September we had a lovely holiday in Crete. On returning, Sharon moved in with me. I'd only had my bachelor pad for six months.

But I must admit it was nice coming home to her at nights. I remember one cold night that winter, I'd been out on a call with Danny. As he dropped me off, about two in the morning, I said, "I can't wait to get in my nice warm bed, with my nice warm girl."

"Sounds good to me mate. See you tomorrow."

A few weeks later, me and Ivano pulled into the yard at lunchtime. Before we got out of the van, the Ayatollah came running out of his office.

"I've got an escape for you down Clarence. Get there as quick as you can. I'll follow."

We were hundreds of yards from Clarence Road, but as we approached the air was full of gas. I looked at Ivens.

"That's a bit rich!"

When we got there, I couldn't believe my eyes. Hackney Council had dug a large hole in the road. One of the guys, using a compressor, had hit the top of the gas main right on the seam, a section of the main had fallen out leaving a hole four feet long, one foot deep. It was just blowing. I can't describe the noise.

I turned to Ivens, "Fuckin' hooray! What we gonna do with this?"

At that point a young fella walked past with a fag on.

"Put that out!" I shouted. "Can't you smell the gas?"

Then I turned to the fitter, Bryan Raymond.

"For fuck's sake block the road off and call the law and fire brigade. One spark and we'll all get barbecued!"

Then we got to work using anything on the van to stop the gas. Bundles of rags, old boiler suits, a donkey jacket, all rammed up the main in a desperate effort. I don't think I've ever sweated so much, mainly with fear.

By now Gatland had turned up with a whole tub of mastic, but was about as much use as a chocolate teapot. Somehow, we managed to stop most of the Gas until the cavalry arrived: a contract mains gang from Dad's yard that had been sent to take over.

Pat Healy came across.

"Hello Tony, how are ya?"

"Fuckin' glad to see you Pat, that's how I am!"

He turned to Gatland.

"Eddie I've some self-centring bags on the van, they'll stop the gas."

"No! You can't use them, it's against the codes of practice."

"But Eddie, it'll stop the gas while we bag it off properly."

"No, definitely not. You shouldn't be carrying them anyway!"

On a job like that the book goes out the window. I turned to Pat.

"So it's okay to shove rags and boiler suits up the main, but not your bags?"

Pat replied, "Sure's the man's a feckin' eedjit!"

Pat's gang took over, so me and Ivano went for a well-deserved pint. To his credit, Gatland mentioned us in despatches and we were both commended, but I'd already decided that, before Christmas, I was definitely going to get 'on my bike.'

'The Knowledge'

In early 1983 I applied, and was accepted, for the Knowledge. In those days, the Public Carriage Office was run by the police. Anyone with a criminal record was rejected. You had to be fit and of good character. They went through you with a fine toothcomb – when you think about it, it's easy to see why.

Imagine I pick you up, and you're going to the airport. You tell me you're off to Spain for a couple of weeks, now I know your house is empty. What's stopping me passing on that information to one of my dodgy mates? Also, at nights, when you're picking up single women, they want to feel safe – always use a licensed cab!

So, I attended an induction meeting at Penton Street. The head carriage officer, Mr Miller, outlined what was expected of us and we each received a copy of the Blue Book. This was a list of four hundred and eighty runs that, when completed, would give you a good knowledge of London. You had to complete this then begin the tests. He was very smartly dressed, and when you made an 'appearance' the COs expected you to wear a suit, as a mark of respect, and to address them as 'sir'.

At the end of the meeting came the bad news: at present the books were full, which meant the standard went up. At that time, the pass rate was only one in ten.

That's not to say only two of us in the room would pass, but for every twenty that signed up only two would go the distance. I decided that was going to be me and someone else! I think most guys knew what they were getting into, but it's true what cabbies say, that if you really knew what it involved, you'd never start the Knowledge.

Sunday morning, and Steve took me out in his cab to do the first three runs. The Blue Book was in no particular order so we did the famous first run: Manor House to Gibson Square, a quarter of a mile down to Myddelton Square, and then on to Golden Square. In the back, I made notes about 'points' along the way, only the basics – theatres, police stations and so on. Steve advised me to keep it brief because, in the end, the points ran into thousands.

It was a good exercise, but there's only one way to do the Knowledge; that's out on the bike seven days a week, in all weathers. In the summer you see loads of fellas out in their t-shirts and shorts, doing a bit and getting a nice tan – they're known in the trade as 'sunflowers'. Come winter, it's a different story, the numbers drop off and it sorts the men from the boys.

A story was going around, of a guy who'd had been doing the runs on the map, but not the bike work. He was on an appearance, being tested.

"Forward Cheapside.

"Forward Newgate St.

"Forward Holborn Viaduct.

"Left Farringdon Rd."

The CO stopped him.

"You went forward Holborn Viaduct, left Farringdon Road?"

"Yes, sir."

"When?"

"About two weeks ago, sir."

"Well I must admire your powers of recovery, because if you went forward Holborn Viaduct, left Farringdon Rod, you must have fallen about thirty feet. Now get out and come back in fifty-six days!"

My father-in-law, Stan, told me about one of his mates. Billy Gross, was up one day with the legendary Mr Finlay, who was bringing in all of his 'stoppers.' Bill was having a nightmare time of it, and at the end his temper got the better of him.

"What's the point of asking me all these stupid questions that you know I can't answer, I only want to drive a cab, not fly a fuckin' helicopter!"

Mr Finlay looked up and smiled as he tore Bill's appointment card in two.

"Thank you Mr Gross. As of now you are officially off the Knowledge."

I'll never forget my first day out on the bike, one Saturday afternoon in February, when the weather was improving. I did the first three runs again, ending with the Garrick Theatre to Broadhurst Gardens, West Hampstead. I had a ride around the area, looking for points, but to be honest I got lost. It was getting dark and I started to make my way home. Where were the lights on the bike? I was lost, it was getting dark and I was still getting used to the bike.

However, after three months I could call the first thirty runs which, with the points, was a lot of information.

Steve encouraged me: "If you can learn thirty, you can do a hundred. If you can do a hundred you can do five hundred. But remember this is just the tip of the iceberg."

Looking back, I realise how that first year I was only playing at it, going out at weekends and on light evenings after work. But it was tough – working on the roads all day, and then three hours out on the bike was like doing two jobs.

In June, exactly a year after we met, me and Sharon tied the knot, but this time is wasn't such a big do. The honeymoon was a week on the Isle of Wight instead of Paris.

As the year came to a close, it was obvious to me that I'd been bitten by the Knowledge bug. I was taking time off work, going Tom and Dick, and spending more time out on the bike. Also, I'd developed that symptom of waking up at night thinking, where's such and such a place? Wherever it was, I'd have to get up and look it up before I could go back to sleep.

By February 1984, I'd completed and could call the Blue Book.

"Right, you think you're the dog's bollocks, now join the school," Steve challenged.

Full of confidence, I took his advice. He told me to get on a good table with guys that were better than me. Pick their brains. That was how to learn – and take a notepad.

That first night was a real eye opener. I sat in with four guys I'd never met. On the table was a list of questions asked at the carriage office the week before.

As the first guy finished calling his run, I said, "Hold up, which way did you go?"

He was shit hot and I made a note of his run. The other three were good too. That night I came down to earth with a bump. Eventually it was my turn and somehow I called the run. Steve told me this was the only way you could practise, being on the spot under pressure.

By the end of the night my new mates had settled me in and told me to put in for my first appearance. I said I didn't think I was ready, but they reassured me.

"Put your papers in, you'll be okay."

On the Friday, the school posted me a list of two hundred questions asked the previous week. As I looked through them, my heart sank. I started listing the points I had to learn. That first week, I only knew forty out of four hundred!

That experience convinced me that if I was going to do this I'd have to go full-time. I'd seen the standard of the guys I was up against. So, I decided to burn my bridges and take redundancy from British Gas. I had a nice few grand in the bank and with Sharon working I thought we'd be okay. Let's go for it!

Next Friday, the points arrived again. The list was growing and I thought I was never gonna be able to keep up with this.

I worked out a routine to plough through them.

Saturday: do the City, when it's quiet.

Sunday: West End.

Monday: North.

Tuesday: South.

Wednesday: East.

Thursday: West.

During the week, I'd do four hours out on the bike, afternoons writing up plus revising fifty Blue Book runs, and Tuesday and Thursday nights at the school. Working like this full-time, I had to improve.

Within a month of joining the school, I got a date for my first appearance.

A few years ago, a cabbie asked me, "What was it about that place that reduced grown men to feeling like frightened schoolboys?" The foreboding atmosphere of the carriage office was unique. Anyone that said it didn't bother them was lying.

Everyone remembers their first 'appearance'. After about ten minutes in the waiting room my name was called.

I followed the CO into his office and took my seat about six feet away from his desk.

After a few minutes reading my file, he looked up.

"Right Mr Davidson, take me from A–B,"

I can't remember the points. I thought about it, and then off I went, very nervous – but managed to call the run.

But, by the third question, my nerves got the better of me, my throat dried up and I couldn't get the words out.

The CO looked up.

"Okay, take a break, clear your throat and carry on."

After about five minutes, I'd answered four out of six questions. The CO made a few notes then looked up.

"Well that wasn't a bad start." They always gave you a bit for nerves on your first time.

"Make another appointment for fifty-six days."

"Thank you, sir."

When I came out the scouts were waiting.

"Who did you have, mate? What did he ask you? That's how the school gathered the points.

"Sorry mate, I can't remember. That was my first time up."

"Don't worry pal, it gets easier as you go. Well done."

At the time the COs were all ex-coppers ranging from Mr Nice Guy to Mr Nasty, with three in between that were firm but fair.

When you've been cabbing a few years, you realise this is a reflection of the general public. You'll meet some very nice people, you'll meet some very nasty people, but most are somewhere in between.

I can't remember my second appearance, but the third stuck in my mind. I had Mr Nice Guy, Mr Lippiat.

I couldn't believe the points he was calling, all basic Blue Book.

"Billingsgate Market, and from there we'll go to St Bart's Hospital." Lovely!

At the end I had almost a full house.

Mr Lippiat looked up.

"Well you seem to be coming along nicely. Do you feel ready to move up a level?"

"Yes, sir."

"Ok, I'll move you on to twenty-eight days. Your next appointment will probably be in two months, but you will be at the higher level. Well done!"

"Thank you, sir."

That day gave me a real boost. I felt I was getting somewhere now.

By the time my next appointment came round, I'd been working hard and making progress with the long lists. I was more confident, but was in for a rude awakening.

My name was called and I looked up to see Mr Shern. His reputation has preceded him. As I followed him into his den, I knew I was in for a hard time.

Mr Shern was six feet four, shaved head, dark glasses, ex vice squad.

For a few minutes he sat there reading my file, occasionally tapping his pen. Eventually he looked up and called the first two points. I didn't know either of them.

"Sorry, sir, I don't know."

Second question.

"The Turf Club to Lyndhurst Road, NW3."

I just couldn't see it. Panic was setting in. Mr Shern looked up.

"You don't know Lyndhurst Road?"

"I do, sir, but I've gone blank."

Luckily I got the third, but come the fourth…

"Royal College of Midwives," (which I knew), "to Brent Park, Neasden."

"Is that part of Brent Cross, sir?"

"No! And don't guess. I don't like it if you guess."

At the end I'd answered two out of seven. Mr Shern shook his head, saying slowly, "You've got a lot of work to do. Come back in twenty-eight days."

"Thank you, sir."

The girl outside gave me my next date. It was three months away!

"Bloody hell, that's a long twenty-eight days!"

"I'm sorry, that's the earliest I've got."

In all my time, I never got twenty-eight days. But three months? Please!

As I came out, I felt I'd been kicked in the balls. As usual the scouts were waiting.

"How'd ya get on mate?"

"Don't ask. I had Shern and he fuckin' slaughtered me."

That morning when I got home an advert came on the radio.

"Come to Tesco's, now at Brent Park, Neasden."

It had only opened at eight that morning, but by ten, Shern was asking me for it.

Over lunch I told the ol' fella. "You know how hard I've been working and he just shot me down in flames, then I got three months. I feel like I'm banging my head against a brick wall."

He came back at me.

"So, what you gonna do? Jack it in? That's what he wants you to do. I thought you had more fight in you than that. Work harder. Go back and beat him!"

"You're right, I'll have a break this afternoon and get back out on the bike tomorrow."

Back at the school the lads said, "That's what it's like on twenty-eights – they build you up, then knock you back down. It's part of the game."

Halfway through the night, a new face turned up.

Most of the guys came down on their bikes and sat around in big jumpers and scarves. This fella was wearing a sports jacket, white shirt and cravat. He looked like he'd fallen out of Burton's shop window.

When he walked in, the parrot house went quiet, as most of us stopped calling and looked up. Stan the Man, who ran the school, got up to meet him.

"Yes, guv, what can we do for you?"

In an upper crust voice he said, "Good evening. Is this where one comes to learn to be a taxi driver?"

"Yes, guv, but as you can see we're very busy tonight. Come back next week and we'll sort you out, okay."

As he left, we all looked at Stan.

"He'll never make a cab driver as long as he's got a hole in his arse!"

The place just fell apart. I don't know if that fella heard, but he never did come back.

As winter set in, the going got tough. I thought I was used to the cold, working out in all weathers, but it was different on the gas. You could work hard to keep warm. On the bike, you just sit there and the circulation goes. First it's your fingers and toes. I remember stopping to take a point once and my hand was too cold to write. When I came in at weekends, Sharon would run me a bath and bring me a hot coffee laced with whisky to warm up. I remember looking down as I sat there shivering, "Where's my dick?" I was so cold that 'Little Tony' had gone up inside me to keep warm!

1984 turned into 1985, but the routine remained the same. One day I ran into my old mate off the gas, Lenny the Lion. He'd taken redundancy at the same time as me and gone into the pub game, but now he too was on the Knowledge. We caught up on some old times. Then he told me about a recent incident.

He'd pulled over in Golden Square to take a point and was sitting behind an ambulance when it started to reverse. Len hit his horn, but it kept coming and knocked him off his bike. The driver came running around.

"I'm sorry, mate, are you okay?"

"Well, yeah, but fuckin' hell mate, what were you doing? Let's have a look at the bike."

Len said he was okay with the driver, but then his mate came round.

"What's happening? What's it all about?

Len told him, "I'm talking to him, not you."

"Well, I think you're making a fuss about nothing."

"Do ya?" Wallop! A big right-hand knocked the bloke spark out.

"'Ere mate, put 'im in your fuckin' ambulance!"

Lenny was one of the hardest men I ever met.

Then I had my best two 'appearances'. First, with Mr Downing, a new CO, younger than the rest. An ex-copper, who himself was on the Knowledge.

In his office that day, a young lady was taking notes.

"As you can see, you've got an audience today, Tony, but I don't think that's going to bother you. Would you like to take your jacket off?"

"No thank you, sir."

I was surprised by his friendly manner and by the observer but he was right, it didn't put me off. I had a blinder.

One of the points was Defoe House, basically just a sign on the wall in the Barbican Tunnel. Luckily, I'd seen it just a few days earlier. I was buzzin' and finished off with Caledonian Road Station to Brookes Club.

"Forward Pall Mall.

"Right St James Street

Set down on the left, number sixty-five."

"Sixty-five?"

"No, sorry sir, number sixty."

"Well Tony, after an average start, your marks have gone sky high. What do you put that down to?"

"Just hard work, sir."

"Well it certainly shows, well done!"

The next one was even better, as I crossed swords again with Mr Shern.

He was pulling out all his stoppers, but that hard work on the points was paying off. As I called the runs, it felt like I was on autopilot. Again, I got almost a full house. That day, I felt ten feet tall, because I knew, and more importantly Mr Shern knew, I was almost ready.

1986 would be one of the best years of my life. Sharon was pregnant for the second time. She'd miscarried a few years earlier, which was tough for both of us, so we waited till she was past the three-month stage before we told anyone. The baby was due in August, so she would finish work in June. Although we were still okay for money, I had to get out this year to start earning some big bucks again.

The next step was to get my twenty-ones or 'threes', as they were known, because then you were up every three weeks and it was downhill all the way.

They say you reach your peak on twenty-ones – and it's true.

Those appearances came round quickly, but my mind felt like a computer. It's an amazing feeling. After years of hard work it all drops into place. After living and breathing it seven days a week, you reach a standard that's impossible to maintain, but that's what's required.

I did four twenty-ones, then got fourteen days. The second time up, my name was called and I looked up to see Mr Miller, the head CO – I knew this could be my Rec, or final appearance.

We covered the usual five or six questions, then he just kept going. This was it, the adrenalin was pumping. At the end, Mr Miller looked up.

"Well you must know that was your Rec. Well done. Put in for your drive and make an appointment for the suburbs."

After nearly three years, I was almost there, but there was still the driving test to pass.

I went across to the school to sort out my 'wangles'. I was like a dog with two dicks when I saw Stan.

"Lovely. Well done, my son! Come down two o'clock Monday, and Sam will take you out."

Your 'wangles' was when you went out in the cab, three or four at a time, to get ready for your 'Drive.' It was a good laugh, going with the lads and Sam, who was an old Jewish cabbie with plenty of tales to tell and advice to pass on.

"You've done the Knowledge and you think you're a cab driver, right?" he asked me.

"Well, yeah."

"Well, you fuckin' ain't! You've done the theory, now you've gotta learn to be a cabbie. That'll take another year or two."

He was right about that.

The cab we used was owned by Ol' Bill, who helped Stan at the school. He was famous for being the most cantankerous old git around. In those days, you had to pass in a manual cab, but if Bill took you out the worst thing you could do was crunch his gears. One fella did and Bill tore into him.

"You c**t! I cannot afford a new gearbox, don't crunch my fuckin' gears!"

In the back, the rest of us tried not to laugh.

There were some real characters on the 'wangles' with me. My favourite was Ramires, a Spanish chef who was one of the worst drivers I've ever seen. One day he was in the chair as we came down by the Sobell Sports Centre. I was in the cricket seat behind him. As he put his foot down, Sam said, "What's he doing?"

"About forty."

"Oi! Slow down, we're going left at the lights."

A bus was pulling out before the junction at Hornsey Road but instead of letting him go, Ramires put his foot down, overtook, then cut across as the bus blasted his horn.

As he threw a left, Sam shouted, "Pull over you fuckin' idiot, you're finished for the day!"

As I took over, Ramires got in the back.

"How'd I do Sam?"

"How'd you do? You've just failed your test. You're doing forty in a thirty zone. Instead of letting the bus go, you fuckin' cut him up!"

"Yeah, but I can't drive with an audience."

"So what you gonna do, drive round empty all day?"

The day of my test came round. I thought I'd done okay and back at the centre I answered all the Highway Code questions correctly. So, I couldn't believe it when the examiner failed me. I thought he was harsh, but had to accept it. Back at the carriage office I made another appointment. It got worse. The next date was six weeks away!

I must admit, when I got home there were a few tears. The baby was due and I felt I'd let Sharon down, but in those days we were very close and she consoled me.

"Don't worry, Tone, just think how hard you've worked. You'll get in next time. You've done three years, a few weeks more won't matter."

I took a few weeks off, picked myself up and started again and the time soon passed.

On August 14th, Sharon woke me at six in the morning.

"I don't think you're going driving today."

Her waters had broken and I had to get her to the hospital.

It brings it all back whenever I watch that episode of Del Boy at the birth, when he's on the gas and air. He's right – it's the good stuff!

Sharon had a hard time in labour, for about six hours. By the end it looked like a Friday night down Hackney Road. A doctor checked with me, "Are you okay, because if you faint, we'll leave you there."

"Don't worry, I'm alright." I thought it was always like that.

Finally, at ten o'clock in the evening, my baby girl, Sarah, was born. When I held her it was love at first sight.

I called in at Mum and Dad's to wet the baby's head. After a few beers I said, "Dad, where's that bottle of Chivas I got you? Let's have a drop of the good stuff."

"No, I'm saving that for a special occasion."

Priceless!

The following Tuesday was my second drive. Since Sarah's birth, life felt in perspective and everything fell into place. At the end the examiner said, "I don't know how you failed the first time. Congratulations, you've passed."

"Have I really? Thank you, sir."

That afternoon at the carriage office I picked up my licence and Green Badge. I'd done it!

Back at the flat we had a party to celebrate and the champagne was flowing! Within four days I'd become a Dad and a London Black Cab driver. It was the best week of my life.

I picked up my first cab that Friday; it was just out of overhaul and shining like a new pin. I felt like a kid with a new toy.

'A Cab to California'

That Saturday felt like when you pass your test and first go out on your own, that's when you learn to drive. Luckily, I didn't get anything difficult it was 'Arrods, Oxford Street, Tower of London, and so on. I enjoyed it, took a few bob and after about four hours I'd eased myself into things, ready to start properly on Monday.

I had a taste of Butterboy Luck as a new cabbie. After a few years on the 'rock 'n roll' it felt great to be earning proper money again. I picked up a French fella going to Heathrow, my first 'flyer'.

After I set him down at Terminal One at six o'clock, I sat there having a count up when Mitch, from the school, pulled up alongside me.

"Hello, Tone, how you doing?"

"Yeah triffic mate. That's my first one up here."

"Are you putting on?" He was asking if I was going onto the rank.

"No, I'm off home, I've had a good day."

He looked down at the wad I was counting.

"I can fuckin' see that! Alright mate, nice seeing you, be lucky."

It's funny, those first few months I ran into most of the guys I'd met on the Knowledge, as a leather-arse. I was putting in the hours to make up for lost time. I even saw

Ramires who'd somehow managed to pass his test but said he hated the job.

There was a fella I picked up off a building site. He was going down to the Geffrye Museum, drop off his tools, then on to another job. As I cut through the back streets of 'Oxton, he commented, "You know your way around 'ere, mate."

"Yeah, it's my manor."

"Was you one of the 'Oxton Mob?"

"No, but I knew most of them."

"You must know my cousin, Jesse James?"

"Yeah, I went to school with him."

We were chatting as I parked up opposite the museum.

"I'll just drop these off, then I'm going on to Mare Street – that okay mate?

"Yeah, alright."

As he went off into the flats, the penny dropped. "Fuckin' hell, he's done me!"

I grabbed my bag, locked the cab and raced through the path after him, but he was well away. I asked two boys, "Did you see a fella come through here?"

"You a cabbie? He does it every night mate."

"Where's he live? I'll give you a few bob."

"Dunno mate."

Typical 'Oxton. They wouldn't grass on him. He'd only done me for a tenner, but it wasn't that. I don't like anyone to take me for a mug.

The next night, I sat around waiting for him, but after half-an-hour, I thought about it. What am I doing here? Just losing more money. That was my first 'runner' and it left a bad taste.

I told all my mates, "If you ever pick him up, do me a favour and give him a slap for me."

One of the lads said, "Just wipe your mouth and put it down to experience." But it put me on my toes. You have to read people. I wasn't the first to be mugged off and I certainly won't be the last.

A few years ago, a Butterboy had his story printed in our trade paper, *Taxi*. He picked up a young blonde in a leather mini-skirt from Marble Arch.

"How much to Leeds?"

She said she was desperate to get home, he agreed to take her for £300. It said that, apart from the money, he'd thought by the look of her that he might end up 'giving her one' and couldn't resist it.

When they got to Leeds, she gave him directions and eventually told him to pull in.

"I'll have to go in and get the money, luv. I'll leave my bag in the back."

After five minutes there was no sign of her, so he went to the house. It turned out to be a bed and breakfast with a corridor where she'd run out the back. He dived into the passenger seat of the cab. Her holdall was full of newspapers. She'd done him like a kipper.

He ended up down the local nick where he gave them a description. The copper said she was a 'working girl', who did the business in London and often found a cabbie to bring her home.

That fella had learnt an expensive lesson, but to give him his due, he was big enough to put it in print to warn the rest of us. The golden rule being: a job like that has to be money up front.

I picked up a geeza in Oxford Street one Saturday morning who, as he got in, just said, "Canning Town." I smelt trouble, I recognised it as someone who'd been in the same clothes too long; he'd been round the clock a few times on the gas.

The roads were clear, but we got caught at the lights by the Old Bailey. He said, "What you stop for mate?"

"The lights are red."

"Yeah, but you could have jumped them."

"No, we're on my licence mate." I looked at him in the mirror – he might as well have had trouble tattooed on his forehead. As I crossed the lights, I pulled over.

"What you stopping for now?"

"This is as far as you go mate, get out."

"If I get out 'ere, I'm not paying you."

"I'm not bothered about that. You look like you ain't got any money anyway. Just fuck off!"

As I span the cab round and headed back up West. I thought I'd rather lose a fiver than end up over Canning Town for nothing. As it happened, just down the road I picked up a couple, with their kids, going to the Natural History Museum. That's more like it, a typical Saturday job.

As the build up to Christmas got going that first year, I was loving it, taking bundles, and there weren't enough hours in the day. As we got into December I was doing seven days a week.

The Knowledge had taken over the past two years, so that Sharon and I hadn't had a proper holiday abroad. She persuaded me to go and see her sister, Sandra, in California, after Christmas, and we booked up to go for the whole of February. Sharon had been a few times before and told me I'd love it; the best part being we'd stay at Sandra's, so we just needed the flight and spending money.

Sandra had been working in the States for six years, as in the eighties it had become fashionable to have an English nanny. At first she worked for Linda and David, who owned a small film company. They must have been doing okay as their daughter, Gemma, went to the same school as Danny DeVito's kids. Sometimes Danny's wife, Rhea, who was Carla from *Cheers*, would pick the girls up from school and had got to know Sandra. She offered her a job with them, and as the money was good Sandra had to go for it.

After a few days, once we'd settled in, we started to get around and visit Sandra's friends. She said Danny and Rhea wanted to meet us and had invited us for dinner. Over the years I've met a lot of famous people in the cab, but it was different going to Danny's for the first time.

Halfway through the night, Danny's best friend Louis Giambalvo turned up and we got chatting.

"Louis, I know your face. What have you been in that I've seen lately?"

"Did you have the *Gangster Chronicles* over there?"

"Yeah."

"I played Al Capone."

Louis is a jobbing actor and turns up in many films, but never really got a big break like Danny did in *Taxi*.

As we left, Rhea invited us to come over again in the week and to use the pool. "It was great meeting you guys."

So, a few days later there we were at the big house. Me, Sharon and the baby, soaking up the LA sun and one of the maids asking, "Would you like a cold drink, Tony?"

There I was, by the pool sipping a cold beer. Talk about 'Oxton boy made good!

That afternoon when Danny got home there was a houseful of women: Rhea, Sandra, Sharon, his sister Angie, who was visiting from New York, and Kathleen, the cook. He came out to the pool and chatted for an hour. I think I was a breath of fresh air to him because, in his position, he was surrounded by people feeding off him and lickin' his arse.

Although I spoke with respect, I never crawl to anyone, and we spoke man to man. He was interested about the Knowledge.

"You have to pass a strict test, right?"

"Yeah, I've done three years and I'm still learning as a Butterboy."

I told him about the first interview when I was told only two of us would make it and how I thought 'that's me and another guy'. He liked that.

"It's a tough job though, right?

"It's okay, you just got to use your loaf."

"Your loaf?"

"Loaf of bread – head."

Danny loved rhyming slang.

I'll always remember how he said, "I know I'm not the world's greatest actor, but I'm one hell of a business man!"

Danny wasn't the only famous face we met. Sandra's friend Hannah worked for the singer, Kim Carnes. One afternoon we popped in for a cup of tea. Kim showed us round her lovely house where pride of place was a baby grand piano. On it were the music and lyrics to 'Bette Davis Eyes'. That song had been a hit all around the world and made her a fortune.

The second week we did the whole tourist thing. When we went to Disneyland, it brought home to me that it's not what you know, but who. Danny's secretary had made a phone call, so we were met by a girl that Sandra knew, who took us to breakfast at the hotel and gave us VIP tickets. They were a freebie for the day, and the best thing was being fast-tracked onto the most popular rides, avoiding the long queues.

When we stopped for lunch I spent time just people watching. Man, there's some fat bastards over there. I always say, if you think you're putting on weight, go to the States, you realise you're not doing so bad after all.

Eight of us went out for a Chinese meal one night. It was one of those buffets where you spin the round table and have a bit of everything – right up my street. I'd had a few beers and was probably talking a bit too loud, telling a few funny stories.

"Tell Louis about that guy from New York," urged Sandra.

Before Christmas, I picked up this fella. He just barked, "Take me to Harrods."

"Are you from New York by any chance?"

"Yeah, howdye know?"

"Just a wild guess, you know it's funny, we share the same language but you use words that we don't, and we use words that you don't, like please and thank you."

"Yeah, that's right."

Went right over his head. As we laughed someone tapped me on the shoulder, a lady on the next table. I think I was keeping her amused too.

"Excuse me, sir, are you a real Cockney?"

"Yes darlin'," I'm the real deal London cabbie."

She was a typical Californian beauty: blonde, bronzed, tits like coconuts.

"Oh man, I love you guys, you're the best! I always use the black cabs when I'm in London."

We were chatting away, when I felt eyes burning into my neck. Sharon said, "You having fun over there, Tone?"

I smiled, "It's been lovely meeting you but, as you can see, I'm with my family tonight. I'd better get back."

I picked up the bill. It was just over a hundred dollars. I showed it to Louis, "Man, if you had that same meal in London, it would cost you £200. I love it here!"

The highlight of the trip for me was going to the Grand Canyon. We stayed overnight in Las Vegas then on up into the mountains.

When we arrived at the canyon it looked eerie. The clouds were low, with the peaks of the mountains poking through.

Sandra suggested lunch. "It'll probably clear later on."

As usual, I'd had a good breakfast of eggs, bacon, and pancakes, so I wasn't very hungry. I just ordered an open beef sandwich. It came up like a Sunday dinner, ten slices of beef, mash, carrots and gravy.

"That can't be mine," I gasped. "No wonder they're all so big over here. If I lived here I'd be twenty stone too!"

Sandra was right; after lunch the clouds lifted and what a sight met my eyes. Looking down into the canyon gave me a real sense of time. It made me think how the seventy to eighty years that we have here is nothing in the great scheme of things. It was a spiritual moment for me, definitely the greatest thing I've ever seen.

Over the years, when I've picked up Americans and got chatting to them, it has amazed me how many haven't been up there.

"What are you going to do while you're here?"

"We're going up to Scotland."

"It's funny, I've been to the Canyon, but never been to Scotland."

Mind you, having been to the England Scotland game at Wembley one year, I met enough Jocks to last a lifetime. Having grown up in 'Oxton, I always considered myself tough, working class. After that day, I realised I was middle class. When I was younger, I'd followed Chelsea away to West Ham and Millwall. I thought I'd seen it all, but that Tartan Army was something else. I don't scare casily, but they frightened me. There's nothing like them this side of hell!

When I got home after a month in the sun, I felt totally relaxed. It had done me the world of good. I was calling everybody 'Man'. When I went back driving, I was letting everyone out before me, but after the wide roads of California, London felt like toytown.

Later that year, Sandra rang and asked us for a favour. Danny was in London for a few days at Claridges. He liked a particular brand of tea that was hard to find in LA. She asked Sharon to make up a parcel and for me to drop it down.

I went down there early Saturday morning, but due to the IRA bombs in London at the time the rank outside was suspended. I pulled up and went to go inside.

"Where do you think you're going?" asked the doorman.

"I've got a parcel here for Danny DeVito. I just wanna drop it off at the desk."

"You're not on mate. You'll have to leave it with me."

"Look mate, I know you've got to be security conscious, but it's not a bomb – feel it, they're teabags."

"I don't care what it is, you're still not coming in."

I can't stand anyone talking down to me like that.

"Look here's his room number. Here's his phone number. You won't believe it, but he knows me. If you don't let me in, I'll call him down to pick it up, but he had a late night last night. I don't wanna disturb him, do you?"

"Go on then, be quick."

"Cheers John, keep an eye on the cab for me!"

A few years later, he was back in town promoting a new film that he'd directed, *The War of the Roses*. His secretary rang Sharon and asked if we'd like to go to the preview. She asked if she could bring her mum and dad.

"No problem."

Stan rang me. "Do you think it's gonna be a showbiz do?"

"I don't know but we better go suited and booted."

A few nights later we pulled up over Hammersmith way and went for a few drinks first. We needn't have bothered. When we got to UIP House, it was a free bar.

I pushed past a fella at the bar, "'Scuse me, mate." It was Ben Kingsley.

"Stan, it's gonna be one of those nights."

I couldn't believe it, as in came Tina Turner, Liza Minnelli, George Michael, and others. It was like a Who's Who. Most of them were in T-shirts and jeans for a quiet night out. "Look at us two," said Stan, "the poorest here, but the best dressed!"

Sunday lunchtime down the pub, I told a few of the locals, "You won't believe who I was drinking with Thursday night?" I could tell they thought, "Oh yeah!" But sometimes the truth is stranger than fiction, as the next two stories will show.

I picked up an old couple, a few years back, going to the British Museum. The old boy was in a wheelchair, his eyes were sunken, a look I'd seen in relations of mine when they didn't have long to go.

The old girl's face was down on one side where she'd had a stroke. They looked pitiful. When we got there I got the old boy down the ramp.

"Thank you, how much do I owe you?"

"Nothing, you just have a good day."

He shook my hand. "That's so kind of you."

As I drove off, I looked up skywards.

"You owe me one, right."

An hour later a black fella called me into an office block and put four ladies in the back.

"Do you know Becket House?"

"Yeah."

"Do you take credit cards?"

"No."

"That's okay, as long as you give them a receipt."

When we got to Becket House, just over Westminster Bridge, they said, "No this isn't it, we want Becket House, Ilford." I said it was a genuine mistake, and reset the clock.

"Don't worry, the firm's paying," they said. When we got over there with £48 on the meter, they told me to give them a receipt for £50." As I drove back to town, I thought, that was my little bit of luck; what goes around comes around.

But it was just the start. For the next few days my luck was amazing. That week I had three jobs to Heathrow, which doesn't usually happen, and I started to think it was lovely, but there was something strange about it.

One afternoon that week, I finished at the City Airport. From there it's a home run up the M11, round the '25' then up the A10 to Hertford. On the way home I pulled over to make a phone call when up came a text message.

"Hi honey, I'm home. Give me a call."

It was my little Italian girlfriend – Maria. She'd been home in Italy for a few months and I'd been missing her. This was just getting better.

I called her and said I'd see her tomorrow. I was buzzing.

Next day, at her house, I gave her a big hug and kiss, then didn't stop talking for half an hour. She looked at me.

"Tony, have you done a line of Charlie?"

"No, I don't do drugs."

"Have you been drinking?"

"No, I've been working, look!"

I pulled out a wad of £300. She said, "You shouldn't carry all that in the cab."

"I've been telling you. That's what I took today!"

I picked that old couple up on a Thursday and it was exactly two weeks after that the run ended. I never knew a time like it in twenty-nine years. Whether they were religious and said a prayer for me, I don't know. What I do know is, it was more than luck.

My brother Steve got his badge a few years before me and has quite a few stories to tell. This is my favourite.

He was in Bond Street at Christmastime, when a woman approached him followed by two black guys. Before she reached the cab, one grabbed her around the neck, while the second tried to rip off her wristwatch.

Steve jumped out and – wallop! Hit the first one in the mouth, putting him down, but busting his own knuckles.

He started on the second one and the woman jumped in. He said there were hundreds of people watching, but no one lent him a hand.

In the melée, the two black guys struggled free and ran off, then a few of the crowd came over.

"Are you alright, mate?"

"What, you want to help me now it's all over?"

The woman thanked Steve and asked was it okay to take her to Hampstead?

"Yes, luv, jump in."

That night, he told me about it. The woman took him in to clean up his hand.

"You should have seen the house, Tone – there was a staircase with rooms off either side."

The lady bandaged Steve's hand, paid him off with a large tip and asked, "Could I have your phone number please? I'm sure my husband would like to thank you."

"I bet you're gonna earn out of this," I said.

Sure enough, her husband rang and asked for Steve's address, as he wanted to put something in the post.

"What did I tell you?"

But being Christmas, the fella didn't send a cheque. Instead a large Christmas hamper – champagne, wine, cheese, everything. Merry Christmas!

The best part of the story came the following summer. Steve picks up this fella and they get chatting. The man said, "I've got a lot of time for you guys. Last Christmas my wife was mugged in Bond Street and a cabbie came to her rescue."

"Hello, Mr Green, I'm Steve Davidson."

What are the odds on that? The true stories are the best. You couldn't make that up, could you?

My best night in the ring

THE TIME OF MY LIFE

IN 'LA', WITH MY 'ITALIAN FRIENDS'

The time of my life

The Taxman

In 1990 Sarah was four and we were looking to buy a house in Chingford, when we got a chance to exchange to a town house at Archway. The only downside was that it was two doors away from Stan and Lil, a bit too close to the mother-in-law.

Having lived in 'Oxton' for so long I wasn't keen on Archway, but we had to go for it; Sharon made it like a little palace, and I could come out straight from home into work.

The first five years I'd been cabbing were a doddle. The late Eighties were the yuppie years, plenty of money about, so most days I could earn whatever I wanted; but at the end of '91 it all changed.

A week before Christmas I drove into Oxford Street from Marble Arch then down to Marks & Sparks and Selfridges – nothing. Oxford Circus – nothing. I went the length of Oxford Street and didn't get a job. It was six p.m. at Christmastime. I couldn't believe it; I'd never known a time like it – that was the start of the recession.

I learnt a lesson that year: don't get in too deep. A lot of fellas fell into the trap when they were earning good money; they'd take out a large mortgage, buy a cab and then, wallop! The bottom fell out and they were in deep shit.

Some guys were working till midnight, driving out to Heathrow then getting in the back with a sleeping bag and waiting for the first flight in the morning. They had to do it, they were so committed.

Although that first recession wasn't as bad as the recent one, it was harder for me.

That year, Sharon had given birth to our second daughter, Jayne; so, with a young family to provide for, I couldn't go home without the bacon.

When I did my books for '91–'92 my figures were low. I'd gone to Stan's accountant, Ken, who pointed out my profits were down.

"Tell me about it mate. But that's what I've earnt."

I wasn't going to declare more just to keep the taxman happy.

The Revenue refused to accept my accounts, and so began one of the biggest fights of my life.

During that time I had many conversations with passengers. A solicitor told me, "You won't win, but you can fight. How long are you prepared to fight?"

"Till hell freezes over. And then I'll fight 'em on the ice!"

When it began I was naïve enough to believe that if you were in the right and told the truth, somewhere along the line you'd get justice, despite the many people telling me, "If the taxman says you're guilty, you're guilty."

They began an investigation that dragged on for six years. Sharon typed up a summary of my case as follows.

Dear Sir/Madam,

My name is Tony Davidson. I am a London cab driver and have been in dispute with the Inland Revenue for the past five years over the tax year 1991-92.

Before moving from London I was the subject of an investigation by the Inland Revenue. In two interviews, I answered all the detailed questions asked of me and provided books of my accounts back to 1986. Despite having my books for two weeks at the first interview the inspector told me she did "not have to look at them". At this point it became obvious to me that the investigation was not being handled in the correct manner. At the end of the first meeting the inspector concluded that "there does not seem to be a problem". I was therefore surprised to receive a further letter, 16th February, from a second Inspector, Mrs Edwards, who having taken over my case now estimated my takings for the year to be over £30,000, a difference of £14,925! At this time I understood the Inland Revenue worked on a basis of £100 profit per £10 of diesel, so using this formula, as my fuel bill was £2,000, the most I could possibly have earned would have been £20,000.

I argued with Mrs Edwards that if in fact I earned £30,000 per year, I would not be living in a two bedroom flat in Islington, driving a C reg rented cab and that her estimate was not reflected in my lifestyle.

Mrs Edwards concluded she could not accept my figures and was referring my case to the tax Commissioner. I replied that I was prepared to go to court as I had told the truth.

Following this meeting my accountant advised me that to go before the Commissioners would be a waste of time as they invariably agree with the Inland Revenue's demands and a better course of action would be to contact my local MP.

After reading the notes of both interviews, my MP Jeremy Corbyn agreed that I had been treated unfairly and wrote to the Inland Revenue on my behalf. However, his letters were met with a negative response.

On 3rd June 1993 Mrs Edwards put my case before the Commissioners who agreed with the Inland Revenue and I was faced with a bill for the year in dispute, plus five previous bills, which I had already agreed and paid. I refused to pay the demand and subsequent bills until this matter was resolved and my name cleared.

In January 1994, myself and family moved to a house in Welwyn Garden City, having been accepted on a Shared Ownership Scheme because on our joint earnings we would only obtain a mortgage of £36,000. Again hardly someone on £30,000 per year!

There followed a break in correspondence until the local tax office contacted me in the summer of 1995 and a third meeting took place at the Luton office. I agreed to begin monthly payments of £150.00 on the tax I owed if the Inland Revenue would review my case, as I maintained my position about the disputed year. However after one instalment, I was informed the Inland Revenue now demanded payment in full and would start County Court Proceedings for £18,000.

On 21st November 1995, I was asked to attend Hertford County Court to see if this matter could be resolved. I was informed that as the meeting was to be informal there was no need to bring my accountant or solicitor.

Consequently, I found myself alone in court, faced by the local collector of taxes, Mr S Kidman, and Registrar, Judge Willers. Totally unprepared, I was asked by the judge to withdraw my defence as, following the

Commissioners' decision, I now had 'no rights in law'. I replied I could not drop my defence because I had told the truth.

I was led by Mr Kidman into a side room where I explained that although I had 'no rights in law' I had no £18,000 either. "What did the Inland Revenue intend to do, make me bankrupt or, worse, imprisonment?" Mr Kidman explained, "No, no." If I was prepared to sign his form, acknowledging that I owed £18,000, the Inland Revenue would agree to monthly payments of £200, an offer I declined!

In the heated discussion that followed I asked Mr Kidman how the hell he thought I had earned £30,000 in 1991-92 during the worst recession in the cab trade for thirty years. At this point, Mr Kidman let slip that the original estimate had since been changed and he seemed surprised when I produced Mrs Edwards' original one.

On returning home, I contacted my accountant who on hearing the morning's events, referred me to a Solicitor who deals in tax matters, as I was intent on taking my case to the High Court. At the meeting with the solicitor I was advised that, although I had a good case and he was prepared to take it on, I would risk my license and possible imprisonment if I lost, that my costs would be high, including his fees of £150 per hour, and I would be better off fighting the case in civil law where the worst outcome was bankruptcy.

At the formal hearing 2nd January 1996 I defended myself to Judge Willers. I argued that the case against me was based on Mrs Edwards' computer estimate that I had earned £30,000 but, following the November hearing, Mr Kidman had informed me this estimate had changed. If the estimate had been changed, it must have been wrong and I could not see how the commissioners' decision could stand.

Judge Willers replied that it did not matter what I thought, as I had no rights in law.

I then asked, if she had done me the courtesy of reading the notes of my interviews with the Inland Revenue and my letter of support from Jeremy Corbyn? The judge replied that she had not received the notes, an MP's letter counted for nothing, and proceeded to pass judgement against me. This amazed me as I had delivered those notes to the court, by hand, two weeks earlier. In June 1996, I was summoned to Hertford County Court under threat of imprisonment for contempt by refusing to make an offer of payment. I agreed to make monthly payments to the Revenue of £200. This was rejected, and my case has since been referred to the Enforcement Office in Worthing. The last correspondence I received was in May of this year: a demand that with interest has grown to over £22,000 and I am now threatened with bankruptcy.

I am determined to fight on against this unjust tax law and have sought help from many people, including two MPs, Citizens' Advice, national newspapers and Tax Aid, who advised me the best solution was to make myself bankrupt. As a matter of principle I have decided against this route and will contest any bankruptcy petition made against me.

As you can imagine, five years of this situation has caused me and my family a great deal of stress and put a strain on my marriage. However, I will continue to fight my case, in any way possible, to clear my name.

Yours sincerely,

Tony Davidson

Through those years I had to retain my sense of humour to keep me sane. In 1996 Mum and Dad followed us to WGC, but within a couple of weeks Mum had a heart attack, followed by a bypass at Harefield Hospital – all this on top of a constant battle with cancer.

Despite everything, she was so strong, the toughest little lady you could meet, and with a heart of gold.

Most nights I'd pop in for a cup of tea. Mum could always tell when something was wrong.

"What's the matter Tone, are you drinking again?"

"No Mum, no more than usual."

"Have you paid your last tax bill?"

"Yeah, a couple of weeks ago – don't worry."

"Alright, I'll see you tomorrow."

The next night she gave me an envelope.

"There's two grand in there to help you out, get the taxman off your back and repay me when you can."

That was my mum, simply the best.

A few weeks later, I'd only been home ten minutes when there was a knock at the door. There stood one of the biggest black fellas I've ever seen.

"Mr Davidson? Bailiffs, I've got a court order that entitles me to kick your door in and start removing goods."

"Is that right? If you do I've got a gun upstairs and I'll fuckin' shoot you! Now what's this about?"

"Your unpaid tax bill."

"What you talking about? I paid that two weeks ago, now I'm gonna get onto the tax office to sort this out."

About ten minutes later he came back. "I'm sorry Mr Davidson, I've been on to my guvnor. There's been a mistake." He held out his hand.

"I don't want to shake your hand, just get off my drive, fuck off!"

The threatening letters and demands were a constant worry for Sharon and me, things like that pull you together or tear you apart. I could just about cope with the sleepless nights, but was drinking too much for my own good. I remember, after another sleepless night, I picked up a fella in Bloomsbury, who asked me for the institute of psychology.

"Where's that?"

"The Maudsley Hospital."

Off we went. I was driving down Fulham Road when he piped up.

"Excuse me, we do seem to be going a rather long way west."

The penny dropped.

"You know why? You want the Maudsley and I'm going for the Royal Marsden."

Instead of going for Waterloo, now I had to go for Chelsea Bridge. You've heard of A Bridge Too Far? That day I was five bridges too far!

I apologised. "Don't worry, guv, we'll sort it out the other end."

We got chatting and I explained why I was having sleepless nights.

He was a psychiatrist so he was sympathetic. As we made our way through Brixton he said, "I've seen parts of London today I never knew existed."

"To be honest, I've seen parts of London I haven't seen for a long time too."

In 1999, the Thursday before Easter, I was summoned to appear at the High Court in the Strand. I left the cab on the rank opposite, and took my bag with all the paperwork. I was met outside by the taxman; an Asian guy with the unusual name of John Thomas. It suited him though as he was a right prick. He looked down at my bag.

"Have you got the money with you?"

"Yeah, I normally carry £24,000 around. What do you think?"

In court I again argued how the Revenue's case against me was based on a faulty estimate that had since been changed.

The judge replied, "This is not the time or place."

"With respect, sir, this is the High Court of Justice – where do I have to go, Strasburg?"

That morning I was declared bankrupt, but I refused to let the bastards get me down. I came out of the court, went back to work, and picked up a couple of Yanks going to the airport.

When I got home, still suited and booted I called in to see Mum and Dad.

She looked at me, "Where you been?"

I hadn't told them because that morning they'd been in London too, at Bart's for mum's six-monthly check up.

"How'd it go, Mum?"

"They've said I've got six months to live."

I just held her as we both burst into tears.

That day was one of the worst of my life.

The Edge

A few months later, all that sorrow turned to joy. The junior registrar had made a mistake.

Mum didn't feel that ill and sought a second opinion from the professor at Harefield who had done her bypass op. It turned out that the mass on her lung was only scar tissue and nothing to worry about. Thank God! She was blessed, and fought on for five more years.

However, in early 2004 she was diagnosed with stomach cancer. This time they were right, it was terminal.

Every night that year, I'd put the cab away, have a few large brandies, then go round to see Mum, who was fighting all the way. I'd try and cheer her up as much as possible, although it was breaking my heart.

When I got home I'd jump in the shower. There was no need to turn on the taps, but I didn't want my girls to see me like that. Then I'd be downstairs, back onto the brandy – my way to ease the pain.

I really needed to talk to Sharon, but we were drifting apart. She wasn't there for me and I was hitting the hard stuff more and more.

When Mum was near the end, she was on a lot of morphine. She looked at me one evening, and said, "Tony, when I'm gone, you'll miss every hair on my head."

She never said a truer word.

On September 4th, she passed away in her sleep. The week after the funeral, no matter how much I drank, nothing eased the pain.

October 18th was Mum's birthday. That Sunday morning we laid some flowers on the grave. When we got home, Sarah went out with her friends. Sharon had taken Jayne to a dance contest. I started drinking at one o'clock and was still drinking at one o'clock the following morning. Next day, I felt too ill to go to work. I was still in bed when Sharon came home for lunch.

"Tone, it's horrible for me to see you like this, let me make an appointment for you to see the doctor tonight."

He prescribed a course of medication to stop me drinking completely for a while.

I was still on the tablets on December 2nd, Sharon's birthday. That afternoon, when I stopped at Lincoln's Inn, I ran into my cousin Tel, another cabbie I hadn't seen since the funeral.

"How are you, Tone?"

"Not good, Tel. I'm on tablets to stop me drinking."

"Oh Tone, you don't need them, you're better than that."

"I'm not, Tel, I've got a problem."

We had a good ol' chat and when I pulled round into Holborn, I picked up an old girl going to Heathrow.

That made my day. When I got home, I thought I needed to cheer up and bought a bottle of brandy.

Big mistake!

It reacted badly with the tablets and a few hours later Sharon found me unconscious, called an ambulance and I spent the night in the QE2 Hospital.

For her, it was the last straw.

The day after Christmas, she said, "There's no easy way to say this, but I want a divorce."

"How can you do this to me? You know what I went through last year. I can't take any more grief. I'll probably drink myself to death."

But I had to stay strong for my girls. I knew, when the divorce came through, I'd be out of the house and wanted to stay with them as long as possible.

It was a difficult time, but in November an angel came into my life.

I'd picked up a beautiful young Italian lady out of Selfridges, going to Cockfosters – lovely! It was about four o'clock and the ride would take me most of the way home.

Her name was Maria. She looked like Christine Bleakley, but with a sexy Italian accent. It doesn't get much better than that. We got talking, had a few laughs and it was obvious there was chemistry between us. Sometimes you meet someone and you just click.

Although she was a lot younger than me, when I got her home I had to ask:

"Don't mind me asking, but can I have your phone number. I'd really like to see you again."

She said she'd like to see me again too. Thank you, God!

By the Thursday before Christmas, I was driving around empty, thinking, "What a fuckin' Christmas this is gonna be." I couldn't find a job anywhere. Then I picked up an obviously gay fella who told me he was a drinking counsellor.

"You're gonna have a field day with me!"

I told him how I felt like going home and taking a load of pills and brandy.

"Don't you dare talk like that! Have you ever thought about turning gay?"

"No mate, I love women too much."

"Are you seeing anyone?"

"Yeah, I've just met a lovely young Italian girl."

"Is she home today? Go and see her, I'm sure she'll know how to cheer you up."

He was right; the first time I kissed Maria I could tell she really liked me. She was so passionate. I explained, "I'm at a really low point, if you see anything in me you like, wait till I get through this divorce. In a few months you'll see the real Tony."

In January, the divorce became final and Sharon made her move. I'd had to put the house in her name after the fight with the taxman.

She got Stan to come round and change the locks one Saturday, when I'd gone to work as usual. When I got home, there were all my clothes boxed up and left on the drive. All my good leather and suede jackets, sitting there for anyone to take. As I hadn't found a flat, I was out on my arse and had to move in with the ol' fella. I felt Stan had stabbed me in the back. We'd been close but I never spoke to him again.

The next few years, it was Maria who kept me going. I cut down on the booze, started eating sensibly and seeing a younger woman made me get back into shape. I was working out and friends were telling me I was looking good. Maria made me feel like a million dollars. One day she complimented 'Little Tony'.

"He's not the biggest I've ever seen, but he's always rock hard!"

"That might have something to do with you, darlin', when I'm in bed with you my fuckin' cat couldn't scratch it!"

She was so good for me and not just the sex, although it was the best of my life. She loved it. One day she said, "I'll still be having sex when I'm seventy."

"Not with me you won't. When you're seventy, the only thing I'll be pushing up will be a few daisies!"

Maria had money and property, here and in Italy. From time to time, especially in winter, she'd go home for a few months, and that's when I knew I had deep feelings for her. When she was away, I ached. I hadn't felt like that since I broke up with June.

But I could never go home with her, as her family were heavy duty, which was the main reason she'd moved here. Also, I wasn't the only man in her life. She had a wealthy boyfriend in the legal profession.

She went home for a family party once. One of her cousins was being released from prison; he'd been given a four stretch for dealing 'charlie', but was let out after a year. She told me her family had paid the judge €60,000. That told me everything I needed to know.

Like all good things, I knew one day it would end. That day came in 2012, when Maria went home for good.

Several songs remind me of her. She loved Paolo Nutini. I told her, "Whenever you play 'Candy', always think of me". I'll always love that girl. She gave me back my pride and the strength to carry on. She sent me a text that I've kept on my phone.

Honey promise me you won't drink remember you are strong, that's what I like about you.
Luv Maria xxx

One day I picked up this young American. He wasn't the sharpest knife in the drawer. As we pulled into Trafalgar Square, he said, "Oh, wow! What's this place?"

"This is Trafalgar Square and that fella up there is Admiral Nelson. When we ruled the world he used to sail round keeping Johnny Foreigner in check. After he beat the French they laid this out as a tribute."

He looked out. "But I thought Trafalgar was a sea battle."

"Yeah, it was."

"So how'd they get the ships in here?"

I couldn't resist it...

"Years ago this was all part of the old port of London. After the battle they reclaimed this bit from the river, paved it over and laid it out like this.

"Oh man, that's awesome!"

"Yeah, mind how you go, Einstein."

I couldn't write this without a few words about that fuckin' *thing* – Livingstone. I blame him for my high blood pressure.

He couldn't wait to get his hands on the carriage office. It was political, like when Maggie Thatcher got in, she was always gonna 'do' the miners. He wanted to make life difficult for us, as he believed most cabbies were slightly right of Attila the Hun.

When he was Mayor I'd see him most nights on the London news, telling everyone how much better the traffic was now he was running things – after I'd spent the day stuck in traffic jams, made ten times worse by him flooding the streets with buses.

The worst was when the bendy buses appeared with his stupid face on the back, smiling like he was taking the piss. A young cabbie told me he'd picked him up one night drunk as a skunk.

"You should have thrown him over London Bridge mate – done us all a favour!"

He was concerned about the lack of drivers from ethnic communities, but there was never any racism at the carriage office. They treated everyone with equal contempt! Everyone got a hard time, but they set a high standard that produced the best cab drivers in the world.

Livingstone brought in a system of positive discrimination and lowered the standard of the Knowledge. I did hear, if he got re-elected, he had plans to rename London, Livingstonia!

In the past ten years, the calibre of drivers has definitely gone down. One day, as I came out of Charing Cross, a young cabbie pulled up alongside me with a job in the back.

"Where's Well Street, mate?"

"Well Street, Hackney or off Oxford Street?"

"Oxford Street."

"You're telling me you don't know Well Street Magistrate's Court? Where'd you get your badge, out of a fuckin' pack of cornflakes?"

Another time:

"Where's the Irish Embassy, mate?"

"How many times you been to the back of the palace? Corner of Chapel Street, there's a building with a big Irish flag on it – bit of a giveaway really!"

That dumbing down really wound me up, no wonder my blood pressure went up so that I'm on tablets for the rest of my life.

I called in to ask my doctor about them.

"These tablets I'm on, do they have any side effects?"

"What do you mean?"

"Remember I told you my girlfriend is a lot younger than me. She's Italian, very passionate and very active on the physical side. Now I don't have a problem with 'Little Tony', but he's not as strong as he used to be. I'm wondering could it be a combination of age and the tablets?"

"It could be the tablets, when did you first notice it?"

"Twice last night, then again this morning."

Seriously though, last year I started working out again, but one day pushed myself a bit too far. I went for a long run and just kept going. I must have done about ten miles when my back went, big time. I was three miles from home on my hands and knees, when, thank God, an off-duty police woman stopped and gave me a lift home.

I was in agony the next day and couldn't move. The doctor came home and put me on strong painkillers. In all, I was off for about six weeks.

When I went back to work I was still in pain, I tried some painkillers from over the counter at Boots, codeine based. They helped, but came with a warning that they could be addictive.

As the weeks passed, slowly I got hooked on them. Six a day became eight, then ten, then twelve, along with a few brandies and beers every night. My old demons were back and without Maria I was once again on the slippery slope and fighting a losing battle.

When I went back to work, I picked up a new cab, a TX4, the best I'd ever had. But at £235 a week it was also the most expensive because of the price of diesel. It was now costing me £400 a week to go to work.

I was talking to my mate Paul who knew I had a problem.

"Paul I've been down twice, and got back up twice, but if I go down again, that'll be it."

"That's bollocks! You're strong. You've done it twice, you can do it again."

To be honest, I didn't share his belief in me. I needed a grand a week to clear £600. With my back problem, I was really struggling. I was deep in debt, getting deeper into depression. I decided this was going to be my last Christmas.

Tony overdosed on 2nd January 2014.

The previous page was going to be the last, but a lady friend of mine persuaded me to finish the last chapter.

As you might have gathered, I have always cultivated a 'hard man' image: the cropped hair, dark sunglasses. Look, like Del Boy once said, "I've played the tough guy for so long, I don't know how to be anything else."

So it's hard for me to bare my soul, but here goes.

My cab licence expired 5th December 2013. I hadn't renewed it, as I didn't plan to be around in the new year.

As usual the ol' fella had gone away for the new year. I decided New Year's Eve would be the night.

I used to love Christmas, but after the divorce I came to hate the whole Christmas thing. I've never really liked New Year's Eve. I think it goes back to when I was a kid. Billy Connelly did a lovely routine about the Hogmanay show on TV, where Jimmy Stewart would jump around in his kilt, singing, "O the mountains over there and the rivers over here".

"Fuck off!"

Then the ol' fella would have his mates in for a party and put on his Singalong with Max LP. Aaagh!

New Year's Eve, and I'd been drinking all afternoon then started on the painkillers. I had four packets, more than enough to do the job.

As I sat there, the Bee Gees were on telly singing, "How can you mend a broken heart?" The tears were rolling down my face. How sad is that?

I had finished a box of codeine, thirty-two pills washed down with brandy and Guinness, when I started throwing up. I had to stop; I felt terrible and hadn't eaten anything for the past few days.

I went to bed about two a.m. on New Year's Day. I felt so ill that I stayed there, only getting up to go to the toilet. I went six times that morning, the fifth was just water, the sixth, just blood. The phone rang a few times, probably people wishing me Happy New Year, but I didn't pick it up.

Thursday morning Steve came round. I kept him at the door.

"Look at the state of you, you look terrible Tone. You're obviously depressed. Why wouldn't you answer the phone? What are you – a coward?"

"No Steve, I'm not a coward. Just do me a favour and leave me alone."

I shut the door and thought, that's it, this time I'm gonna do it.

I started drinking and taking the pills again, I threw up but this time carried on. By lunchtime I'd done two packs of codeine, sixty-four tablets, plus six Lyprinol to round it up. I lay down and went to sleep, hoping to never wake up.

However, the ol' fella came home later that afternoon and found me semi-conscious. He took one look at me and called an ambulance. I was rushed to the QE2 Hospital and spent the first hours in A & E with a drip in my arm, throwing up. Then they moved me up to a ward, where things took a turn for the worse.

They'd just connected me to an ECG when my heart went like a clenched fist. When it started running, my heart felt like it was going to burst. The monitor was bleeping like crazy.

A nurse told me to take deep breaths, try to relax.

"Relax, I'm having a fuckin' heart attack!"

I looked up at the light above me and thought, this is it – I'm going.

But after about ten minutes the pain eased and my heart rate slowed down. By now a doctor was there to make sure I was okay.

The little nurse that looked after me that night was lovely.

"Try to drink plenty of water, the more you drink the quicker you'll flush your system," she suggested.

"I'll do that – the one thing I'm good at is drinking!"

I spent the next few hours drinking water and pissing like a horse. But again, things took a turn for the worse.

I never found out, until afterwards, that codeine is opium based. The amount I took was taking effect and I started to hallucinate. I've never done hard drugs, but if ever there was a bad trip, this was it. My vision became blurred with reds and blues on either side. I started seeing things. The fella opposite was very ill. I saw someone get into bed with him.

I buzzed for the nurse.

"Nurse, someone's just got in bed with the fella opposite."

"No, he's okay, don't worry."

As I looked at her, she seemed to have the face of an angel but, suddenly, it turned to the face of a demon. I held my head in my hands.

"Fuckin hell! I'm going out of my mind. I feel like I'm dying and I'm in between heaven and hell."

"You're okay. You're still on the ward. You're very tired. Lie down and try to rest."

As I lay there, it was like my worst nightmare. I lost all track of time. I couldn't take any more and began to pray.

"Dear Mum, dear God, help me through this night. I swear I'll never drink again."

I looked up; the ward was dimly lit by one ceiling light. It became brighter and a beam of light shone down to the floor. In the middle of the beam was the face of an angel, and I burst into tears.

A few minutes later, I buzzed for the nurse. I sat on the edge of the bed. When she came over I held both her hands.

"I've just seen something, but I'm stone cold sober. Can I ask you, do you believe in God?"

"Yes."

"So do I." I cried again.

"Lie down and try to sleep."

I was hallucinating but, that night, something in me changed. I started to feel calm. I lay back down, exhausted. The ward was on the sixth floor, the wind and rain lashed against the window. I'd just dozed off when up went the lights. It was six a.m., breakfast time.

Before she went off duty, my nurse came round to see me.

"How are you feeling, Tony?"

I just feel so ashamed. I'm so low that I'm not in the gutter – I feel I'm in the sewer. Thank you for looking after me last night. You really are a little angel. I'm sorry for swearing, I was out of my mind."

"I know, don't worry, you just keep fighting and I'll see you tonight."

That morning a doctor came along on her rounds.

"How are you feeling? Do you mind if I ask you some questions?"

She had some students with her.

"After last night you can do what you want. Poke me with pointed sticks if you like!"

They put an old boy in the bed next to me. They drew the curtains but I couldn't help overhear that they were fitting a catheter.

"Now this is going to hurt. Are you sure you can't use a bottle?"

"Yes, unfortunately the good Lord didn't bless me with a long enough penis."

I thought, what a poor old sod – he must have a little one.

Fridays in hospital it was fish 'n chips for lunch.

"Would you like some?"

"Please. I've not ate anything for the last few days."

I sat up and had just put on the salt 'n vinegar, when the old boy next door let rip and farted out loud. For fuck's sake! But I had to laugh. I still had my sense of humour.

That afternoon the ol' fella came in with his old lady friend Iris, followed by Sarah and her fella Ryan, who said, "Tony, this really is it mate. You can never drink again."

Then Steve came in, with his usual brand of tough love.

"Tone you've got to sort yourself out, cos when Dad's gone, if you're in the gutter I won't help you. I'll leave you there."

"Thanks Steve, that's just what I wanna hear right now."

I had a heart scan and a chat with a psychiatrist, who booked me in for counselling. Next day, they let me home and I went to see my doctor. I'd come out of my state of melancholy; the depression had gone, together with my urge to drink. I asked her,

"How is it I've stopped drinking, with no medication and no withdrawal symptoms?"

She said, "I can't explain it. Maybe that night you did, literally, see the light."